MW00575575

Daniel Roars Today

End-Time Prophecies
Affecting You

This writer does not believe
in the rapture.

Daniel Roars Today

End-Time Prophecies
Affecting You

by John Klein
with Michael Christopher

Lost in Translation
PO Box 8224
Bend, OR 9770

For speaking and conference information:
Lost in Translation
PO Box 8224
Bend, OR 97708
www.lostintranslation.org

Published by Selah Publishing Group, Bristol, TN
© 2015 by John Klein with Michael Christopher

Cover design by Katie Klein
email: katie@katiekleinsmm.com
URL: katiekleinsmm.com

Unless otherwise indicated, all Scripture quotations are from *New American Standard Bible®* (NASB) © 1960, 1977, 1995 by the Lockman Foundation. Used by permission.

Additional Scripture quotations are from: *The Holy Bible, New International Version* (NIV) © 1973, 1984 by International Bible Society, used by permission of Zondervan Publishing House.

The Amplified Bible (AMP) ©1965, 1987 by Zondervan Publishing House.

The Holy Bible, King James Version (KJV)

Printed in the United States of America
ALL RIGHTS RESERVED

No part of this publication may be reproduced, stored in a retrieval system, or transmitted in any form or by any means – electronic, mechanical, photocopying, recording, or otherwise – without prior written permission.

International Standard Book Number: 978-1-58930-299-0
Library of Congress Control Number: 2015904284

This book is lovingly dedicated to
Evan and Sarah Klein and the daughter we are expecting with great joy,
and to
David and Jessica Ryals and their daughter Isabelle.
May God bless them with the grace He gave to Daniel to be
bright lights and bold voices to their generation.

Other Books by the Author

Available at lostintranslation.org

Lost in Translation: Rediscovering the Hebrew Roots of Our Faith
(John Klein and Adam Spears with Michael Christopher)

Lost in Translation: The Book of Revelation through Hebrew Eyes
(John Klein and Adam Spears with Michael Christopher)

Lost in Translation: The Book of Revelation: Two Brides — Two Destinies
(John Klein and Adam Spears with Michael Christopher)

The Key to Your Weather Forecast
(John Klein)

Anatomy of the Heavens: God's Message in the Stars
(John Klein with Michael Christopher)

Contents

Acknowledgments

I am so grateful to my partner in writing, Michael Christopher, who first thought we had the potential to put our life teaching into books and who has worked tirelessly and faithfully to see this vision come to pass. Without Michael there would be no books.

Thank you to Garlen Jackson, our publisher, who has been patient and kind and given great advice. Selah Publishing Group has made the process efficient and smooth.

Thank you to Katie Klein, our 22-year-old, for our beautiful cover and for putting this book on Kindle.

Thank you to my wife Jodi for the many hours she spent editing and cleaning up some of the details. She plays a key position in refining my thoughts and making them clearer.

Finally, I'd like to thank my kids: Tyler, Maegan, Chad, Katie, and Cassie. They make life rich, full of laughter, and extra meaningful. Thank you for helping us come up with the title for the book and for the fun we had around the table on September 28, 2014, going through Tyler's other suggestions:

A Timely Mauling
Daniel in the Lion's Din Two: Double the Lion, Double the Lyin'

Get the Lead Out of Your Tush and the Iron Out of Your Feet
A Furnace for Everyone
It Doesn't Look Good: God's Got Lions, and You're Not Daniel
Humanity: Golden Potential, Iron Clad Failure
Shadrach, Meshach, and Abenda-Uh-Oh

John Klein
Bend, OR

Foreword

This is the fifth book I've worked on in collaboration with John Klein. That collaboration began in 2002 with what was intended to be a single tome on the book of Revelation. But over the next ten years that "single tome" gradually expanded into three separate volumes, the first one focusing on the background of Revelation and the next two focusing on the text of Revelation itself.

However, once you've thoroughly examined the book of Revelation you can't possibly retire from the field without a comparable study of the book of Daniel. To quote from a popular song from the 1950s, those two biblical masterpieces "go together like a horse and carriage." And to quote once again from that same song, "you can't have one without the other." Except that in this instance I would substitute the word "understand" for the word "have."

In other words, you can't truly understand Daniel until you understand Revelation, and you can't truly understand Revelation until you understand Daniel. Here's just one example, taken directly from the text ahead that illustrates what I mean:

> In our previous publications – for example, when we studied the book of Revelation – we noticed a consistent

construction pattern in which God would present material in groupings of seven. We saw seven letters to seven churches, seven seals on a scroll, seven trumpets being blown from the temple, seven bowls being poured out on mankind, seven thunders that left us all with questions . . . and seven angelic proclamations. . . . Is it any wonder that we find that same format in the book of Daniel? Knowing that there are seven visions, or dreams, that Daniel writes about in his original scroll, does this also convey the idea of completion as well?

To most readers, that last sentence introduces what is without question the most electrifying revelation in the coming chapters. Given the way events have been lining up over recent years, those seven visions that God gave to Daniel could absolutely come true in many of our lifetimes.

In other words, it is essential to understand the book of Daniel if you want to understand some of the most important events that are converging right now. If you believe that the Bible is the true word of God, you need to read this book as well. I guarantee that it will vastly expand your understanding of what God Himself, in His mercy, has given to help us comprehend what's ahead.

Michael Christopher
Bend, Oregon

Before You Begin...

I n this book we have broken the chapters into two parts. The first section, separated by a different style font, will include "fictional" characterizations of certain portions in the life of Daniel, detailing how he might have confronted various trials that came into his life. The rest of each chapter will contain a detailed examination of the book of Daniel itself.

These introductory sections will be filled with many facts, but they will also include some fictional "additions" that we believe will help all of us understand the book of Daniel – and Daniel himself – much better.

Also, in the past we have tried to write from a Hebraic perspective, bringing added insights into biblical passages. In this book we want to continue doing that, but we want to add a little flair this time. We wanted to stretch our imaginations a bit in our approach to writing about the prophecies in the book of Daniel.

Daniel himself is a unique character, and his book is even more unique. He is one of the few people found in the Bible for whom God never includes any negative comments. He's almost a biblical standalone in the praise he continually receives and the confidence God has in him with respect to his personal responsibilities in life. God shows this same confidence in Daniel's reliability, stability, and the quality of the relationship He had with him.

As a result, Daniel is an important biblical character. He also recorded an important section of history, which is especially significant now because the time period we live in at the moment has a lot in common with the time period the story of Daniel tells us so much about. God also gives Daniel prophecies that are specifically for our day.

Daniel lived in a time when God had had enough with the disobedience of Israel and the rest of the world – so much so that He finally brought the judgments He had promised ancient Israel if they disobeyed Him. He'd given them centuries to get it right, but they had repeatedly rejected their Maker.

Daniel's life starts at the very end of the time period in which Israel was still a nation – but was only a shadow of its former self. About a century earlier the northern ten tribes had been conquered by Assyria, and about 28,000 of the members of those ten tribes had been exiled to Nineveh, the capital of Assyria, which lay in the Mesopotamia Valley on the shores of the Tigris River. At the same time, many more thousands of conquered Israelites had been allowed to remain in the northern portion of Israel, but they lost the freedom they enjoyed in the past.

Daniel was a young boy, probably in his early teens, when the two southern tribes, which made up the nation of Judah, were invaded as well. Just a few years after the death of Judah's King Josiah, King Nebuchadnezzar of Babylon invaded and conquered the remaining Promised Land of Israel that God had given to the Israelites centuries before. Common to ancient invaders after they conquered new nations, King Nebuchadnezzar exiled the very best people, which many times included the royalty, the leaders of commerce, and the wise men. And Daniel was included in the excommunicated group.

Today, we are on the threshold of a similar situation, geopolitically and morally. We are now at a moment in history when the world as we know it could easily be turned upside down by war. All over the globe, including the United States of America, moral values are decaying rapidly, the consequences of which are seen everywhere in our society. These consequences include higher levels of crime, destruction of the family, and much political corruption.

As with Israel of old, God will also bring the same promised judgment upon this world and the United States for its rejection of Him. It's interesting to note that the ancient Babylonian opposition that came against Israel in earlier times is the same opposition that will come against all of God's people at the end of time, that being Babylon.

By looking at Daniel as a real person living a real life, perhaps we can learn some important principles that will also apply to our own lives.

One final note. There is a lot of scholarly speculation today on how to properly pronounce God's name, which He told the Israelites to use in reference to Himself. We've represented this by YHWH in our text. After researching we have settled on "Yahuwah" as the proper pronunciation, but not dogmatically.

1
An Overview

T he old prophet awoke with a start. He had fallen asleep at his desk again, his head lying on his crossed arms. But the results of his hard toil over the past few weeks lay before him now. Maybe he did deserve a bit of a break. The records were complete.

Standing up, he rubbed his eyes and admired what he had accomplished. He took the large scroll containing the records and laid it gently on the floor. Beside it he spread a soft rug so he could lie on his stomach and get a bit more comfortable. Propping himself up with a pillow, he slowly rolled through the Aramaic and Hebrew script he had meticulously used to record the messages God had given him over the last 70 years.

These godly messages – seven in total – had been the entire focus of his work. The scroll was made of animal skins, perfect for recording information the writer wanted to preserve for a long time. Over many decades these skins would eventually become brittle and unreadable. But before that time he anticipated that someone would make a copy, keeping his God-given visions, dreams, and historical records available for all who would come after him.

Ideally, the people who would live during the fulfillment of the words he'd been given would also have plenty of access to what he had just written down. God meant for these words to encourage the believers who would come along in later years, but they were also warnings and witnesses against those who refused to heed His counsel. The old prophet's God seemed to be very concerned with providing plenty of evidence about His existence and His plans.

Oh, and did He ever have plans! He wanted everyone to make Him their closest friend, but doing so had to be mankind's choice, not His. However they chose, their decisions would not have any impact on the ultimate fulfillment of God's intentions. The only thing men and women could decide would be which side they would choose to be on.

The old prophet's upstairs room looked out onto the king's courts. He had been closely associated with the two governments that had ruled the known world of his day. First it was the Babylonians – King Nebuchadnezzar, to be exact. Nebuchadnezzar had led his armies to the prophet's home and had put it under siege. Unable to defeat the army that oppressed them, the people of the nation of Judah and its capital, Jerusalem, led by King Jehoiakim, were finally overwhelmed and conquered. And, as was the custom of conquering kings in that era, most of the wisest men and women, with the most promising potential, were exiled by King Nebuchadnezzar and taken back to the capital of his own kingdom, Babylon.

As he lay on the rug the old prophet recalled that long trip. With his hands tied in front of him, he'd been pulled along with other exiles by a rope attached to a smelly camel. The caravan, traveling along the King's Highway, took him into lands he had never visited before, including lands that he mostly wanted to forget. All he could remember was the dust and the blowing sand. Oh, and that heat!

The knowledge that he might never be free again – that he might spend the rest of his life as a slave to some unknown master – didn't help either. As if the heat alone were not bad enough, those tormenting thoughts blazed through his mind. In his former life he had been a student, studying to become a worthy servant of the Most High God – someone who would someday help lead his own people. He would certainly experience a bright future.

A new reality came into view as he realized that all his previous preparations back in Jerusalem could be for naught. He was now destined to spend the rest of his life in an entirely different way.

But now, with the scroll spread open in front of him, he chuckled and shook his head at his lack of faith. He should have known that his God would not have given him such potential – and gifted him with such high hopes – only to let him be exiled to a foreign land with nothing positive in his future. Yet he eventually began to see God's infinite wisdom at work in his new life. Arriving at such an understanding wasn't entirely easy. But the information he had learned as a youth was nothing more than that . . . just information. His God wanted him to learn how to put it all into practice in his daily life.

His new life here in Babylon had brought trouble, stress, and finally an argument that developed out of a fit of anger. He remembered that day vividly, having blamed God for all his troubles. For a time he believed that God had abandoned him and didn't care about him. Ultimately he almost betrayed the very relationship he thought he had with his Creator.

If only he could have seen what the future held. If only he could have seen in those early years the destiny God had in mind for him and the responsibilities God would entrust to him. Trust, insight, faith, and dependability were the attributes God first required of him. But meanwhile he also needed to learn a few additional things. He needed somewhat different qualities to see himself through the difficult times ahead, including stability, an ever-present focus on his God, patience, humility, and the faith to stand up for his beliefs in the face of those who could snuff out his life with a word. These were the lessons that then lay before him.

Meanwhile, over the past few years a new ruler over the known world had emerged. King Cyrus of the Medes and Persians had ended the kingdom of Babylon. This new king's courts were the ones the old prophet's window looked down upon now. But he fondly recalled that at first he had served King Nebuchadnezzar.

When he originally won the freedom to walk in Nebuchadnezzar's courts, the hanging gardens – already recognized by many as one of the seven wonders of the world – were a sight to behold. In the course of time King Nebuchadnezzar developed a special relationship with the old prophet, whose name was Daniel. The king even began to rely on him for counsel and guidance.

In fact, the king eventually elevated Daniel to the second-highest position in his court as a direct result of the confrontation the king had with God. This became the turning point in Daniel's and Nebuchadnezzar's relationship. The king saw in Daniel something different – something that the others who served him didn't have. Maybe it was loyalty, maybe a certain selflessness, maybe something someone could learn only from the hand of God.

But it didn't start out quite so grand. Along with several of his friends, all exiles from Jerusalem, right after he arrived in Babylon Daniel was placed in King Nebuchadnezzar's palace and given food, the very same food served to the king. On the surface that didn't sound so bad. But Daniel knew that most of the world, and especially those who could afford it, would readily include items in their diets that God had said were not "foods" acceptable for His people. They were things God said would bring defilement if eaten.

And that was the start of the tension. Why was he always being asked to stand out, to be different from everyone else? Why couldn't his God just allow him to blend into the background and not be perceived as a troublemaker? Especially by the king, no less.

As it turned out though, after asking to eat a diet of his own choosing, he and his companions were singled out from among all the others. In fact the king said that in matters of wisdom and understanding, Daniel was ten times more insightful than all others who were serving him.

In our previous publications – for example, when we studied the book of Revelation – we noticed a consistent construction pattern in which

God would present material in groupings of seven. We saw seven letters to seven churches, seven seals on a scroll, seven trumpets being blown from the temple, seven bowls being poured out on mankind, seven thunders that left us all with questions (because John, the author of the book of Revelation, wasn't allowed to write anything about what they meant), and seven angelic proclamations.

Is it accidental that we find this consistent use of the number seven by God? Or did He set the tone in the very first chapter of Genesis by creating and then resting in a total of seven days? He didn't need to rest, but he did so as a model showing how we should live our lives.

However, God also intended to convey to us the meaning of the number seven – *completion* and *perfection*. So, whenever you run across "seven" in the Bible, God wants to convey those two important concepts. In the book of Revelation we find all of these sevens bringing us to a completion of His work, that being the end of the Age of Man and the reinstitution of the rule of God's creation by King Messiah.

Is it any wonder that we find that same format in the book of Daniel? Knowing that there are seven visions, or dreams, that Daniel writes about in his original scroll, does this also convey the idea of completion and perfection as well? We believe it does.

Seven Visions

Daniel's seven visions are as follows:

1) The statue
2) The tree
3) The last four beasts/kingdoms
4) The two-horned goat
5) The seventy-week prophecy
6) The antichrist and his archetype, Antiochus Epiphanes
7) The last 3 ½ years

In contrast to the rest of the books in the Old Testament, the book of Daniel is unique because it is composed of both historical accounts and prophecies. The other books tend to contain either one or the other. Or, sometimes they are poetic expressions of knowledge and wisdom and heartfelt love for their maker, which is what we find in Psalms and Proverbs.

The Hebrews most often refer to their Scriptures, which Christians call the "Old Testament," as the *Tanakh*. Tanakh is an acronym for *Torah, Nevi'im*, and *Ketuvim*. These last three words are the Hebrew names for each one of the three main groupings of books found in the Old Testament. In English the meanings of these three words are *law* (i.e., principles for holy living), *prophets*, and *writings*.

Most people falsely assume that the book of Daniel fits into the Nevi'im, the prophetic section in the Tanakh, but the ancient Hebrews put Daniel in the writings (Ketuvim) section. Either way, the unique construction of the book of Daniel gives us a wonderful blend of history contrasted with harbingers of the future.

One more thing that's helpful to know. Many times in His Word, God uses a fascinating technique to convey ideas, visions, and plain old information. First He presents an overview, then He isolates one section of that material and gives more detail. In the context of prophecy He'll give us a sweeping panoramic view of what lies ahead, and then He will focus on a narrower band of time about which He then delivers a lot more detail. For example, consider Genesis 1 and 2. Chapter 1 is a panoramic view of what God did during the first week of Creation. Chapter 2 is an elaboration of day six.

Or, take an example from the opposite end of the Bible. In Revelation, we are introduced to seven events known as the seven seals. In Revelation 6, God gives us a broad view of events over a period of time. Then He narrows His focus in chapter 8 by focusing on the last seal, giving us much more detail about what's going to happen, in contrast to any of the other six seals.

Dreaming but Not Drifting

[handwritten: ? doesn't match what the actual scripture says — p.34 - alluding to previous kingdoms]

The first dream in the book of Daniel does exactly the same thing. It begins with a panoramic view of the seven evil kingdoms Satan has used to attempt to rule and reign over God's creation, then focuses on the last four.

Most of the information, however, is pertinent to the very last of the seven kingdoms, while much of the remaining six dreams, or visions, also focus on the last evil kingdom. The last kingdom, of course, deserves the most coverage because Satan's end game – which is to completely rule the entire earth in defiance of God – will come to a different kind of ending than what he had hoped for.

Each one of these seven evil kingdoms, most of which have already played their parts in the history of this world, was created in the mind of Satan. These seven kingdoms are as follows:

1) **Babylon**, led by Nimrod, whom Abraham confronted and defeated in order to possess the eastern lands that God had given to him. Nimrod's empire only diminished from this point forward. *(handwritten: (King Amraphel, Gen 14, 2250–1860 BC) right foot right calf of Neb's statue (?))*

2) **Egypt**, the kingdom that put Israel into bondage. Egypt's mastery over the known world at that time came to an end, after the ten plagues, when Pharaoh also lost the best of his army in the depths of the Red Sea. *(handwritten: (1850–1200 BC) Statue's upper left leg (?) 1446 BC - Exodus from Egypt)*

3) **Assyria**, which conquered and exiled the ten northern tribes of Israel. The exile of the Israelites was the pinnacle of the Assyrian rise to power. Their power only decreased from that point on. Within 100 years Assyria was no more. *(handwritten: 722 conquered 10 north tribes; Right arm and chest 3rd menoral branch; 612 BC Neb's father Nabopolassar takes control)*

4) **Babylon revived**, this time led by Nebuchadnezzar, who conquered the two southern tribes of Israel, together known as Judah, and exiled them back to Babylon. Babylon also came to its end when it confronted the God of the Israelites. This is recorded in the story of the handwriting on the wall, in which the king of Babylon disrespectfully used the accoutrements *(handwritten: Judah? Benjamin)*

(handwritten: EVIL MENORAH (p.37))

of the temple of God. That very night the king died, and the kingdom of Babylon ended.

5) **The Medo-Persians**, who conquered Babylon and released the Israelites from their exile.

6) **Greece**, led by Alexander the Great, who conquered the known world in ten short years, including the land of Israel. He subjugated that world to his own religion, called *Hellenism*, which was a form of paganism known for rampant sensuality.

7) **Rome** reached its pinnacle of strength and decreased only after destroying God's temple in Jerusalem. As we will learn, the seventh kingdom will have two phases. One phase has been fulfilled at the hands of ancient Rome. The second phase of the Roman Empire is prophesied to come to its end by confronting God, this time in the Holy of Holies in the third temple.

In each one of these kingdoms the ruler's primary goal was worldwide conquest and subjugation, through military force, intrigue, and sometimes religious persecution, especially against those who followed the ways of *YHWH* as echoed in the nation of Israel. These seven kingdoms had rulers that we believe were strongly influenced by Satan, as suggested by the similarities between their goals and the techniques they used to reach those goals, plus their similar perversions.

For example, Nimrod's Babylon spawned the polytheism that became the foundation for the world's false religions. From that point on, each subsequent kingdom took on Nimrod's pagan religious structure and built onto it. A fascinating study could be done of the evolution of each one of these kingdoms' so-called "gods" and how they are related. Here's one example, as highlighted by Nimrod's goddess of fertility.

Astarte and Helen – Pagan All the Way

Her name was *Astarte*, from which the Greeks got the model for the goddess they called *Helen*, who was a copycat of Astarte. In the Bible we see numerous references to Asherah poles[1], a type of wooden pole associated with the worship of Astarte, from whose name we get our word *Easter*.

Yes, the word Easter has very pagan roots. During Easter celebrations it's common for adults to buy little bunnies and hide Easter eggs for their children to discover. Since Astarte was the goddess of fertility, the custom of using bunnies and eggs as ancient/modern symbols of fertility continues but has nothing to do with the actual day on which the Lord resurrected.

Unfortunately, these types of celebrations could be considered an a front to God. Satan has substituted a pagan name and pagan customs for the actual festival on which the Messiah arose: Firstfruits. In an amazing correlation and fulfillment, Yeshua (the Hebrew name of Jesus) died on the first festival, Passover, was buried on Unleavened Bread, and resurrected on Firstfruits. The most important events in Yeshua's life on earth occurred on ancient festivals. And so will the final prophetic events leading up to His Second Coming.

Pagan gods and goddesses are actually fallen angels, better known as *devils*, all fighting for the love, attention, admiration, and worship of mankind. Of course, this is exactly what God desires from man. But, Satan is in the business of subverting God's goals and accomplishing his own.

Two Kingdoms

Ironically, in some ways Satan's and God's goals, on the surface, are almost one and the same. Both will attempt to set up a one-world government and rule from Jerusalem. Both will set up a standard for people to live by, and both kingdoms will honor and elevate to positions of authority those who align with their leader's principles.

Satan's final kingdom, the second phase of the seventh evil kingdom we spoke about earlier, will go to battle against God at His Second Coming as the real King replaces Satan's kingdom with His own. This battle we all know as *Armageddon*, in which Satan will suffer his almost-final loss.

The seven visions of Daniel give us a mirror of the book of Revelation. While Revelation focuses on the blessings and the curses of God – the wedding between Himself and His people versus the judgments that God will bring upon nonbelievers – the book of Daniel focuses on Satan's agenda. Throughout the history of man, through tyrannical means revealed via Satan's attempts as detailed above in the seven evil kingdoms, Satan has sought to promote his own perverted agenda. All this will someday culminate in one last failure, in which he will challenge the very Creator of the Universe for the right to rule.

Through Daniel's insights we can discover the agenda, the characteristics, and the overall construction of Satan's final efforts at the end of days. Studying the book of Daniel through these lenses will expose the motivations and the heart of Satan himself and make us wiser in dealing with the authority he is about to exert over the earth.

2
The Statue
(Daniel 2–3)

Over the past few years a new conqueror had become the ruler of the entire known world. King Cyrus of the Medes and Persians ended the kingdom of Babylon and set Darius as the new governor over the city of Babylon. This new king's courts were the ones Daniel's window looked down on now, even as the old prophet slowly got up from the floor where he had been examining his newly finished scroll.

Suddenly the prophet realized how time had gotten away from him. He needed to be on his way, for he didn't want to be late for dinner – especially dinner served up by the king's attendants. As a long-term friend of both King Nebuchadnezzar and King Cyrus – and their families – Daniel was a regular guest at the kings' table. There he was able to share his dreams and visions, for both kings took special interest in Daniel's prophecies and their meanings. But all three men were confounded by "the secret."

As we all know, whenever someone tells you about the existence of a secret, yet won't tell you what that secret is, it drives you crazy. That is the effect that this secret had on the two kings and Daniel. Despite all of their speculations and imaginings they knew they really didn't have a clue. God had hidden it from them, at least for now.

Nebuchadnezzar was the first king to invite Daniel to his table. Daniel had earned that honor by telling the king his dream and its interpretation concerning the statue made of four metals. That was the plus side of the story. The negative side involved all the hatred against Daniel that it caused. You would think that saving everyone's neck would have earned Daniel a bit of favor with all the magicians whose necks were on the line. But no, it had just the opposite effect. Extreme jealousy rose up in all of these pagan mystics. The king had threatened them with death if they could not tell the king his dream and its interpretation, and only Daniel had been able to do this. Daniel has saved their lives.

Daniel's scroll, which still lay on the floor, had not included much about the trouble he'd had with the king's court, however. Why add to the problems that already existed? Plus, the point was that God had done a great miracle that night. Giving glory and honor to Daniel's God was exactly the opposite intention of the king's other sages, who were actually representing the enemy.

After hearing the demands of the king with respect to the dream and its interpretation, Daniel had run back to the dwelling where he lived. Back to his friends, some of the Hebrews that he knew from home, Jerusalem. They were also exiles, now serving in the court of Nebuchadnezzar. Three of them were named Shadrach, Meshach, and Abednego, but these were their given names in exile. They were family now. Their real names, their Hebrew names, were Hananiah, Mishael, and Azariah.

That evening and late into the night, they prayed together that their God would reveal this mystery to them and save their lives. Sure enough, as miraculous as it was, Daniel received the exact dream that the king had envisioned the night before. Despite their awe over what God had done, solving the mystery was actually the start of all their problems.

Many people suppose that Nebuchadnezzar was a tyrant, and maybe he was. But there were times when the old prophet thought that the king had a relationship with the God of the Hebrews. This was one of those times. He couldn't believe the king's response. In addition to falling down and worshipping Daniel after hearing the dream's interpretation,

King Nebuchadnezzar proclaimed that Daniel's God was the God of all gods and Lord of all kings. Now Daniel knew why God kept putting him in awkward positions. In having Daniel stand out God could reveal who He really was . . . through Daniel.

To Daniel's great relief, God had come through again. He realized that his God had indeed given him exactly the same dream as the king's and the interpretation as well. Daniel learned a great lesson that day. If he was obedient to his God and stood out by showing up and speaking up, Elohim also showed up, with great power, to give His servant insight, wisdom, and authority to minister . . . even to King Nebuchadnezzar!

What was an even greater miracle was the king's reward. Daniel stood in front of the king absolutely stunned, not knowing what to say next. But he need not have worried. Nebuchadnezzar had set Daniel's three friends over the affairs of the province of Babylon. Then he made Daniel himself the ruler over the whole kingdom of Babylon and chief of the governors over all the wise men.

However, as wonderful as all that seemed, it introduced a serious problem. The king's magicians couldn't handle what had happened to Daniel. This upstart young kid was now the governor of them all? In fact, Daniel wasn't even sure that HE could handle it! He didn't have that kind of experience. Maybe they were right. They were older, much more equipped and prepared for the responsibilities of such a high position.

An idea gradually came to mind later that evening, when he was back home alone. Maybe he should have turned down the king's offer and suggested one of these other wise men instead. That would certainly have made some points with these troublemakers. At the time, standing before the king, he couldn't think. Now he knew why the other lesson God had for him to learn was trust. Daniel would certainly be relying on God to fill the shoes of his new position, but from then on it had to be moment-by-moment and day-by-day.

Daniel knew that the worship he received from the king that day was completely undeserved. It wasn't him, but God who knew so much and was therefore the real source of the insights Daniel gave to the king.

One problem that Daniel didn't have was pride. He knew his limits, and they were many.

At the same time he could see the hand of God at every turn. In both the good and the bad, God was working all of this out according to His will. Most of the time, even though Daniel couldn't see the reason for what was happening, he knew that there was indeed a plan, and it was intended to be for Daniel's good. God was using him and his friends to reveal Himself to King Nebuchadnezzar.

Getting angry at God because of trouble was just nonsense. Why should Daniel attack the very One who loved him and was working everything out for him, in spite of Daniel's inability to perceive the overall plan? Rather, faith and trust was the dual lesson before him.

He took comfort in that knowledge, but it didn't help much with respect to the secret. What was this "being that would come" all about? The king and Daniel had discovered some facts about this person. They knew that he would come near the end of the world, just before Yeshua would take His place on His throne in Jerusalem and rule the earth along with His bride. They also knew that he was not good. King Nebuchadnezzar and Daniel both wondered how God would respond to those who would be deceived by this man.

But what they didn't know was how this eventual intruder would fool so many, allowing him to come to power in the first place. How would he unite the entire world, and what sort of being would he really be? Worst of all, they couldn't figure out what impact he would have on God's people. Would they all go through these times of trouble, or did God have something else in mind?

It was getting late and Daniel was keenly aware of his desire to spend these last few minutes before he went to bed with his best friend, Yahuwah. Spending time with his God had become a daily routine. But he didn't just set time aside each day to talk with God, he had also learned to take God with him wherever his daily activities took him.

Later that night, as Daniel contemplated his life, he thought, "What could be better than a full belly, a friendship with the Creator of the universe, and to hear God say, 'You have done well and have earned the reward I have set aside just for you before you were born. Rest easy tonight and take comfort in the peace I give you.'"

Nebopolassar, ruler of Babylon from 627 to 605 BC, put Jerusalem to siege in the last year of his life. He did this through his son, Nebuchadnezzar, who was the commander over Nebopolassar's army. Unfortunately, while waiting for news of the results of the battle over Jerusalem, Nebopolassar died. Nebuchadnezzar returned to Babylon as soon as he heard of his father's demise.

In the second year of Nebuchadnezzar's reign he had an extremely unusual dream which troubled him greatly. The biblical text doesn't go into detail but alludes to the idea that Nebuchadnezzar was dealing with his father's conjurers, sorcerers, and advisors as a source for all mystical communications from the spirit world. But Nebuchadnezzar obviously didn't trust them very much, as revealed by the way he chose to have them interpret this same dream.

When prophets and/or magicians are recorded as interpreting a dream or a vision in historical or biblical texts, they are usually told what the dream or vision was. In this case, because Nebuchadnezzar apparently wasn't so sure of these pagan mystics' reliability, he approached the situation a bit differently. He asked them first to recount his dream and then to interpret it. And, of course, this didn't go over very well. It's one thing to interpret a vision you've heard someone else describe; it's a whole 'nother thing to interpret one that you haven't heard anything about. However, from the king's perspective, his unusual request would certainly validate his mystics' veracity . . . or not.

Separating the Men from the Boys

Meanwhile, all the mystics begged the king to reveal the dream before they interpreted it because they knew that what he was asking was way beyond their capability. While they were arguing with the king, he decided to give an order to destroy all the "wise men" of Babylon. So the decree went out from his throne that all the wise men and magicians should be slain, which included Daniel and his friends.

As everyone who has ever read the book of Daniel knows, Daniel intervened by providing the king with a detailed description of his dream, followed by its interpretation. What God was revealing through this dream were the details and instructions concerning four kingdoms, one of which was Nebuchadnezzar's current kingdom and three more that were yet to come.

Each of the next three kingdoms that followed would destroy the previous one. The last of the four kingdoms would culminate in the coming of the one true God, the true Creator, and the setting up of His kingdom.

In establishing His kingdom, God would have to confront and destroy Satan's kingdom and purify the earth. Nebuchadnezzar's vision revealed and described, in chronological order, the four kingdoms that were yet to come and alluded to the three kingdoms that had already come, which existed before Nebuchadnezzar's time. In total, this equaled seven evil kingdoms.

Clues to the Final Kingdom

God often has very interesting ways of getting information to mankind. Daniel 2 is a prime example. God starts with a panoramic overview of information, usually presented in chronological order.

This is precisely what He did in the first two chapters of Genesis, as indicated earlier. The first chapter gives us an overview of His work of creation, and brings it to a conclusion with God resting on the seventh day. Genesis 2 follows by giving us more information about a passage of time contained within that seven days – in this case, the work that He accomplished on day six. By presenting information in this way, God is giving us a clue as to what is the most important information. Thus, chapter two of Genesis tells us all about the creation of man and

34

the first interactions between man and his creator. Of course we know that man is the apple of God's eye and is the pinnacle of God's creation.

Daniel's first vision works the same way. All the subsequent visions highlight aspects and give more details about the kingdoms that are first revealed by this panoramic view. We will then discover the most important bit of information God wants to reveal about all of these evil kingdoms. *The last kingdom will be a combination of all the kingdoms that came before.* And, it will wreak the most havoc over not just the world of ancient times, which consisted of areas in and around the Middle East, but will include destruction and control of the entire world.

These prophecies – and the details about how the leaders of each one of these kingdoms will rule and reign over the people – are important because they reflect qualities and attributes of the final king. And the fact that all these kings are tyrannical reveals to us the compound layering of evil that the final kingdom will embrace and include. By studying each kingdom we can then identify the main attributes of the final one.

The First Vision in Daniel

The dream Daniel interprets in chapter 2 symbolizes all seven kingdoms of the Dragon (i.e., Satan) but gives detail about the final four kingdoms. The fourth kingdom of the seven evil kingdoms is the head and the other kingdoms are represented by branches (or limbs) on the left and right sides of the statue's body. Here's the text, doubtless familiar to all students of the Bible:

> [28]"However, there is a God in heaven who reveals mysteries, and He has made known to King Nebuchadnezzar what will take place in the latter days. This was your dream and the visions in your mind while on your bed. [29]As for you, O king, while on your bed your thoughts turned to what would take place in the future; and He who reveals mysteries has made known to you what will take place.

35

[30]But as for me, this mystery has not been revealed to me for any wisdom residing in me more than in any other living man, but for the purpose of making the interpretation known to the king, and that you may understand the thoughts of your mind. [31]You, O king, were looking and behold, there was a single great statue; that statue, which was large and of extraordinary splendor, was standing in front of you, and its appearance was awesome.

[32]"The head of that statue was made of fine gold, its breast and its arms of silver, its belly and its thighs of bronze, [33]its legs of iron, its feet partly of iron and partly of clay. [34]You continued looking until a stone was cut out without hands, and it struck the statue on its feet of iron and clay and crushed them. [35]Then the iron, the clay, the bronze, the silver and the gold were crushed all at the same time and became like chaff from the summer threshing floors; and the wind carried them away so that not a trace of them was found. But the stone that struck the statue became a great mountain and filled the whole earth.

[36]"This was the dream; now we will tell its interpretation before the king. [37]You, O king, are the king of kings, to whom the God of heaven has given the kingdom, the power, the strength and the glory; [38]and wherever the sons of men dwell, or the beasts of the field, or the birds of the sky, He has given them into your hand and has caused you to rule over them all. You are the head of gold.

[39]"After you there will arise another kingdom inferior to you, then another third kingdom of bronze, which will rule over all the earth. [40]Then there will be a fourth kingdom as strong as iron; inasmuch as iron crushes and shatters all things, so, like iron that breaks in pieces, it will crush and break all these in pieces. [41]In that you saw the feet and toes, partly of potter's clay and partly of iron, it will be a divided kingdom;

but it will have in it the toughness of iron, inasmuch as you saw the iron mixed with common clay.

[42]"As the toes of the feet were partly of iron and partly of pottery, so some of the kingdom will be strong and part of it will be brittle. [43]And in that you saw the iron mixed with common clay, they will combine with one another in the seed of men; but they will not adhere to one another, even as iron does not combine with pottery. [44]In the days of those kings the God of heaven will set up a kingdom which will never be destroyed, and that kingdom will not be left for another people; it will crush and put an end to all these kingdoms, but it will itself endure forever.

[45]"Inasmuch as you saw that a stone was cut out of the mountain without hands and that it crushed the iron, the bronze, the clay, the silver and the gold, the great God has made known to the king what will take place in the future; so the dream is true and its interpretation is trustworthy." (Daniel 2:28–45)

The two feet, legs, and arms plus the head form the evil kingdom menorah, an idol/monster menorah of seven lights representing seven kingdoms that have become world powers throughout history. These seven kingdoms, or kings, are referred to in the passage below and are under the control of the Dragon, Satan:

> "The seven heads are seven mountains on which the woman sits, [10]and they are seven kings; five have fallen, one is, the other has not yet come; and when he comes, he must remain a little while." (Revelation 17:9–10)

The woman here represents the pagan polytheistic religions. These were created by Nimrod, the ruler of the first of these evil kingdoms, Babylon. These verses reveal that for a time these pagan religions will be the driving force over the empires (represented by seven mountains) as seen by her position on top of these mountains. But this control and authority will be only for a time. The beast, the ruler of the last of the seven empires, will replace her in the end (Revelation 17:16).

In the first vision Nebuchadnezzar saw a huge statue made of four different types of metal. It had a head of gold, shoulders and arms of silver, belly and thighs of bronze, lower legs of iron, and feet of iron mixed with clay. This vision focuses on Nebuchadnezzar's kingdom and the three additional kingdoms that will come before the return of the Messiah. However, its allusion to the three additional kingdoms comes via the left and right side of the statue. In fact, the statue's legs, thighs, arms, and head actually take the form of a menorah.

As fully explained in *Lost in Translation: Rediscovering the Hebrew Roots of Our Faith*[1], the very first menorah was the one that God instructed Moses to build for the tabernacle in the wilderness. This lampstand included seven branches, all originating from a common core, terminating in wells of oil that were lit to provide light for the inner court of the temple. It stood five or six feet high and was made of gold. The oil flowed from reservoirs located along the center light, called the *shamash*. The oil itself was fed to the seven lights through the hollow branches.

The six branches (three on each side of the central shamash) represent man, for he was created on the sixth day. Thus man's number is six. In a perfect state God wants us connected to Him. On the menorah He is represented by the central light, called the shamash, which is the Hebrew word for "sun," and metaphorically stands for God because He is the Light of the World.

The six arms that connect to the central shamash were hollow. The oil flowed through these hollow arms feeding the lights at the end of each arm, representing how God wants our relationship to be with Him. He is the one who provides the Spirit that should be flowing through us so that we, as ambassadors for Him, also act as lights to the world.

The fact that there are seven lights on God's menorah also reveals the purpose that He has for man. The number seven in Hebrew represents *completion* and *perfection*. At the end of the age He will come for a completed and perfected bride.

The Three Evil Kingdoms That Precede Nebuchadnezzar

Nebuchadnezzar is the head of the statue he saw in his dream, but three evil kingdoms come before him.

1) Babylon was ruled by Nimrod (also known as Amraphel). Per ancient Jewish records King Amraphel of Genesis 14:1 was actually Nimrod, the ancient king of Babylon who authored the confrontation between God and Satan at the Tower of Babel[2]. This kingdom ruled the known world from about 2250 to 1800 BC. It existed concurrently with Abraham, and thus we see Abraham confronting Nimrod/Amraphel, the king of Babylon, after Amraphel defeated the kings of the Jordan Valley (Genesis 14). From the military confrontation between Abraham and Nimrod, Nimrod's kingdom declined in power. This kingdom was represented on Nebuchadnezzar's statue as the right foot and calf.

2) From around 1850 to 1200 BC, Egypt comes to the forefront as the world's leading power. The statue's right upper leg corresponds to Egypt which used a combination of military force and economic resources to supplant Babylon as the ruling world empire during the time of Joseph, around 1850 BC. During a worldwide famine Egypt took full advantage of the reserves created by Joseph, enslaving the Middle East in exchange for food (Genesis 47:14–20).

We're all aware of the story of the Israelites working in Egypt as slaves under the rule of the pharaoh and the confrontation with God that finally "Let His people go" in about 1446 BC. The plagues that came from the hand of God, via Moses, culminated in the destruction of the Egyptian army in the Red Sea. The Egyptian Empire began its decline.

3) The third evil kingdom was that of the Assyrians. The pinnacle of their empire occurred around 700 BC when they conquered

and exiled the northern ten tribes of Israel. From that point on the Assyrian Empire declined, culminating in the complete destruction of their nation. Their kingdom ended at the hands of Nabopolassar, Nebuchadnezzar's father, the king of Babylon in 612 BC.

The third menorah branch, or the right arm and chest, represents this empire. The Assyrians exploited Egypt's weakness wrought by God's plagues prior to the exodus and began to rise in power around 1200 BC. Over the next six hundred years, Assyria became the new ruling power in the world. The Assyrians invaded the land of Israel in 722 BC and conquered the ten northern tribes. A couple of decades later they confronted King Hezekiah and made Judah into a vassal state. Recall the confrontation between Sennacherib and God, when God destroyed Sennacherib's entire army (II Kings 19:35). This was probably the turning point in Assyria's supremacy, and from that moment on their power diminished. Ninety years later they were confronted by the new rising authority, revived Babylon, which destroyed them once and for all.

The Next Four Kingdoms

The next four sections of the statue represented Nebuchadnezzar's kingdom and the final three that were yet to come.

4) Nebuchadnezzar's own kingdom, revived Babylon, was represented by the head of gold. This kingdom rose to power in 612 BC, with Nebuchadnezzar becoming king in 605 BC. Nebuchadnezzar was the son of Nabopolassar, a Chaldean chief who in 626 BC led a revolt against Assyrian rule, proclaimed himself king of Babylon and, in alliance with the **Medes** and Scythians, succeeded in overthrowing the vast Assyrian Empire and destroying Nineveh, its capital, in 612 BC.

612BC - 539 BC

Nebuchadnezzar, as crown prince, was given command of the Babylonian army, which he used to harry the remainder of the Assyrians in northern Syria. Nebuchadnezzar thus became head over the fourth evil kingdom, a revived Babylon, around 600 BC. The vision in Daniel 2 pictures this king as the golden head of the statue, putting him as the shamash, the center light, of the evil kingdom menorah. Like Nimrod before him, Nebuchadnezzar attempted to subjugate God to man by assimilating Him into the world system.

5) The Babylonian Empire was completely destroyed at the hand of Cyrus, the king of the Medo-Persians, in 539 BC. The Medo-Persians reigned from 539 BC until 333 BC. Cyrus appointed Darius as governor of the conquered area. Historians believe that Darius was Cyrus' general who seized Babylon and killed Nebuchadnezzar's descendant, Belshazzar, after the Lord predicted the king's demise via the handwriting on the wall the night before the city fell to the Medo-Persians (Daniel 5: 26–28; circa 539 BC). This fifth kingdom is represented by the arms and chest of silver (on the left side of the monster menorah.) One of the best known Medo-Persian kings, King Ahasuerus, better known as Xerxes, presided over the drama involving Esther and Haman, in which Haman nearly destroyed the Jews.

6) Greece is represented in the statue by the thighs and belly of brass or bronze, placing it sixth on the monster menorah. Alexander the Great of Macedonia, who came to power to help unify and control the Greek Empire, became the next world conqueror. As general and king, he swept through Egypt, Asia Minor, Syria, and Mesopotamia, conquering the Medo-Persian Empire and seizing control of the known world.

Beginning with the expansion of his kingdom beyond the borders of Greece in 332 BC until his death, Alexander was in command for only 10 years. But the kingdom that split apart at his death, into four separate states, ruled the world until 63 BC.

After the Medo-Persians allowed the Israelites to return to their land and rebuild Jerusalem and the temple, Alexander the Great put them back into bondage. Greece introduced moral and spiritual corruption into the Jewish people through what became known as Hellenization.

7) In 63 BC the Romans became the dominant world power and ruled until their western capital, Rome, fell in 476 AD.

Their eastern capital, Constantinople (modern-day Istanbul) survived for several additional centuries.

In one form or another, the Roman Empire has never been completely eliminated by an invading army. It has continued to survive to this day. This final kingdom, Rome, is represented on the statue as the legs of iron and feet of iron and clay. Rome, in its representation as the legs of iron, was ruled by the Caesars, destroyed the temple, oppressed the Jews, and scattered them throughout the world. The second phase, the feet mixed with iron and clay, is the one remaining evil kingdom that has yet to manifest. This kingdom will be identified by having a king that is described in the Bible as both a beast and dragon. This king will be assisted by the false prophet and the whore of Babylon. These beings will once again attempt to corrupt and destroy all of God's people.

Main Players in the Last Evil Kingdom

Satan = the Dragon

The beast = the antichrist, the false messiah, a Nephal indwelt by Satan

The false prophet = Abaddon indwelling the body of a Nephal

The whore = a devil who attempts to deceive the world by false religion

---

These are the tyrannical, despotic, evil kingdoms of Satan that have risen and fallen throughout time. Again and again the Adversary has attempted the same scheme, in repeated endeavors to usurp God and destroy His people.

Babylon – First, Last, and Center

Keep in mind that Babylon plays a unique role as the first, center, and last kingdom of the seven evil kingdoms. The first kingdom of Satan's seven is Babylon, and the last kingdom is Rome, which Revelation 17 calls Babylon. Nebuchadnezzar's Babylon is in shamash (fourth) position as the head of the three previous and three subsequent kingdoms.

So Babylon takes the first and the last and the middle (shamash, or sun) position on the menorah that displays Satan's seven evil kingdoms. This is reminiscent of God and His kingdom. God calls Himself the first and the last (Isaiah 44:6; Revelation 22:13), and claims to be our source of light (the shamash, which lights the other lamps). In John 8:12, He claims to be the Light of the World.

In the Bible, gold represents God. We see many of the items in the tabernacle made of gold, the symbol of royalty, which God certainly is. And, as Satan continues to try to steal God's identity, so he does with this statue. By claiming that his kingdom, represented by Babylon, is the first, the last, and the center made of gold (the head), Satan exemplifies a copycat effort to attempt to fool mankind. Satan's goal is to make mankind believe that HE is the creator God and the controller of the universe.

Common Things Among the Kings

Kings who ruled over these evil kingdoms had some things in common. Most thought that they were gods themselves. For example, Alexander the Great thought he was a demigod, born of a woman and a god.

Some of these kings died in the same way. Some of the details of their deaths have been lost to history, but several died of syphilis, which we all know is a sexually transmitted disease that results in a very painful and excruciating death. If you've read our *Lost in Translation*[3] series, you know that each of the seven bowls of judgment poured out on the earth amazingly represents one of the symptoms of the progressive stages of syphilis.

It's interesting to note that most of the tyrants who ruled the world as kings of these evil empires thought of themselves as descended from divinity and therefore as if they *were* a god. Their mythologies promoted the belief that they were descended from gods (i.e., via gods mating with human women) and strikes a parallel chord with the Bible.

Genesis 6:1–4 describes fallen angels as mating with human women and producing Nephilim, or "men of renown."

We would like to report that "living" Nephilim are entirely creatures of the distant past – that maybe a few new ones were born after the Flood, but that the Israelites wiped them all out when they conquered Canaan and they've never been reproduced since then. But of course we can't certify any such thing. Consider just a few clues . . .

When various speakers in the B'rit Hadashah [New Testament] talked about "false prophets" they used idiomatic Hebraic terms that referred directly back to earlier terms for the Nephilim – for example, "men of old" and "men of renown." Obviously, Nephilim were still around in those days. Consider what the Lord tells us in II Peter 2:12–19:

> [12] But these, like unreasoning animals, born as creatures of instinct to be captured and killed, reviling where they have no knowledge, will in the destruction of those creatures also be destroyed, [13] suffering wrong as the wages of doing wrong. They count it a pleasure to revel in the daytime. They are stains and blemishes, reveling in their deceptions, as they carouse with you, [14] having eyes full of adultery that never cease from sin, enticing unstable souls, having a heart trained in greed, accursed children; [15] forsaking the right way, they have gone astray, having followed the way of Balaam, the son of Beor, who loved the wages of unrighteousness; [16] but he received a rebuke for his own transgression, for a mute donkey, speaking with a voice of a man, restrained the madness of the prophet. [17] These are springs without water and mists driven by a storm, for whom the black darkness has been reserved. [18] For speaking out arrogant words of vanity they entice by fleshly desires, by sensuality, those who barely escape from the ones who live in error, [19] promising them freedom while they themselves are slaves of corruption; for by what a man is overcome, by this he is enslaved.

The NIV translation of the Bible renders the last three verses of the above (17–19) as follows:

> [17]These men are springs without water and mists driven by a storm. *Blackest darkness is reserved for them.* [18]For they mouth empty, boastful words and, by appealing to the lustful desires of sinful human nature, they entice people who are just escaping from those who live in error. [19]They promise them freedom, while they themselves are slaves of depravity – for a man is a slave to whatever has mastered him. [Italics added]

Further support comes from Daniel 2:43–44:

> [43]And as you saw the iron mixed with miry and earthen clay, so they shall mingle themselves in the seed of men [in marriage bonds]; but they will not hold together [for two such elements or ideologies can never harmonize], even as iron does not mingle itself with clay. [44]And in the days of these [final ten] kings shall the God of heaven set up a kingdom which shall never be destroyed, nor shall its sovereignty be left to another people; but it shall break and crush and consume all these kingdoms and it shall stand forever. (AMP)

Here, Daniel talks about the statue he sees in his vision, and refers to the four evil kingdoms, represented by gold, silver, bronze, and the feet that were made of iron mixed with clay. But Daniel is saying something else, too – something often missed. According to Hebraic symbology, clay is the sign for man. Indeed, the word *adamah* (whence comes the name "Adam;" thus, within the first man's name is a direct reference to where he came from) literally means "soil," and iron is the sign for angels operating on the earth. Therefore, within the kingdom of the beast, Daniel is prophesying that there will once again be sexual activity between women and devils. As in the days of Noah, mankind will be sexually interacting with fallen angels (Genesis 6:1–4). These angels were the same ones who were locked in the abyss during Noah's era, by God, and who will also be released by Abaddon (Revelation 9:2–3).

In other words this familiar passage from Daniel is prophesying that fallen angels will once again be having intercourse with women and producing offspring as they did in the days of Noah, just before Yeshua comes back for the final time. Ancient Rome represented the calves of iron on the statue in Nebuchadnezzar's dream, but what about the feet of iron and clay and the ten toes? This kingdom is yet to come and represents the second phase of the ancient Roman Empire. It is rumored today that the world will be divided into ten sections, and it is possible that the leaders of each will give their authority to the beast, the false messiah, in fulfillment of end-time prophecy (Revelation 13, 17).

The Rise and Fall of the Seven Evil Kingdoms

These seven evil kingdoms have many things in common, including what brought on their downfalls. When each of these kingdoms grew powerful enough they would confront God's people. God rises up to protect His people, while Satan's plans have always included subjugation, destruction, or deportation.

Abram rescues Lot, and Blessed by Melchizedek

The confrontation between Abraham and Amraphel (Nimrod) in Genesis 14 occurred at the pinnacle of Nimrod's kingdom. From that point on, Babylon became weaker while Egypt grew more powerful. Egypt, the next evil kingdom, never recovered from the ten plagues brought on by God's judgment on Pharaoh.

Assyria, after destroying and exiling the northern ten tribes to Nineveh in 722 BC, tried to do the same to Judah. Hezekiah, the Judean king ruling from Jerusalem, saved his land and his people from the Assyrians by worshiping the one true God. As a result of the confrontation between Hezekiah and King Sennacherib, 185,000 soldiers of the Assyrian army were found dead in their camps the next day (2 Kings 20:35). The Assyrians never recovered, and ninety years later they lost what was left of their kingdom to the Babylonians.

In 539 BC, the end of the Babylonian Empire occurred when Belshazzar, a descendant of Nebuchadnezzar, defied God by slandering Israel and

Israel's authority in public. The finger of God literally wrote Belshazzar's judgment. That night his kingdom fell to the Medo-Persians.

The movie *300* depicted a battle between Greeks and the Medo-Persians which took place soon after Haman, one of the highest officials of the Medo-Persian kingdom, tried to destroy all the Jews in the land. His efforts were thwarted and God's judgments were revealed in the results of the battle with Greece. From this time onward the Medo-Persians became weaker while the Greeks grew more powerful.

Alexander the Great, the leader of the united Greek city states, conquered the known world in 322 BC but died ten years later. His kingdom was split into four parts and ruled by his four generals. One of the last ones to rule was Antiochus Epiphanies, whose death, due to what historians believe was syphilis, occurred shortly after his confrontation with the Jews in Israel, where he desecrated the temple and defied God. His army, huge as it was, was embarrassed and defeated by an untrained band of Jewish farmers and priests, known to history as the Maccabees.

This vacuum allowed the Roman beast to rise to power in 69 BC. The Romans, through military force and political intrigue, controlled, manipulated, and slaughtered the Jews and exiled the survivors from their own land. In the Bar Kokhba rebellion in AD 132, Rome confronted the Jews one last time and destroyed the Jewish nation, dispersing the people all over the world and eliminating most of the Jewish population in Israel. The nation of Israel wasn't re-established until 1948.

During the intervening 1,800 years, various world governments continued to pursue the Jews throughout the world, wherever they could find them. We've seen the same thing in pogroms such as the Spanish Inquisition and the slaughter of the Jews in Russia, France, England, and other countries, culminating in the rise of Adolf Hitler. Unfortunately, the last manifestation of the Roman Empire, the one made of iron and clay, will again attempt to attack Israel and exterminate the Jews once and for all, as prophesied several times in the Bible.

It's also interesting to note that, with respect to all of these evil empires, most of the kings, rulers, or founders themselves were said to be the offspring of a human woman and a "god." Unfortunately, the same will be true of the ruler of the last evil kingdom. It will have a leader known as the antichrist, or false messiah, who will be part man and part devil, impersonated by Satan himself proclaiming to be the God of the Bible.

Losing Our Way

Look at what Rome accomplished by yanking Christianty under its wing. It essentially stripped out most of the Torah-based ideas that were widespread and prevalent before Rome messed with it. Sadly, in the centuries that followed, Satan has further attempted to subvert the true worship of God, in ways that have resulted in forms of religious expression that have very few connections to the Bible. Thus we have the *form* of religion but not the *power*.

Unfortunately, the former emperor of Rome, Constantine, one of the Ceasars of Rome, is portrayed today as a great Christian leader who incorporated Christianity into his kingdom. Nothing could be further from the truth. He did it to control and pollute the kingdom of God. For him it was better not to feed the Christians to the lions but to water down their religion until it bore little resemblance to what Yeshua had taught. This also added to the rift between Christians and Jews.

Constantine's method was also much more effective. In Satan's kingdom there is no room for Jews even as he enfolded the religion of Christianity into his own empire in a perverted sense. Satan deluded the Jews until they missed their Messiah, and he deluded and corrupted the Christians until they lost the Torah-based roots of their beliefs.

Did Nebuchadnezzar Turn to God?

Some propose that Nebuchadnezzar, through the process of having his dream revealed and interpreted, converted to faith in the one true God. This opinion is derived from the last four verses in Daniel 2:

⁴⁶ Then King Nebuchadnezzar fell on his face and did homage to Daniel, and gave orders to present to him an offering and fragrant incense. ⁴⁷ The king answered Daniel and said, "Surely your god is a God of gods and a Lord of kings and a revealer of mysteries, since you have been able to reveal this mystery." ⁴⁸ Then the king promoted Daniel and gave him many great gifts, and he made him ruler over the whole province of Babylon and chief prefect over all the wise men of Babylon. ⁴⁹ And Daniel made request of the king, and he appointed Shadrach, Meshach and Abednego over the administration of the province of Babylon, while Daniel was at the king's court. (Daniel 2:46-49)

In verse 47, the king says "Surely your god is a God of gods and a Lord of kings." Through Daniel's faith and willingness to risk his own life and reputation, he might have had enough of an impact on the king to cause him to actually want to know Daniel's God. This should spur us on as well, to do the same when God is moving in our hearts to witness to others.

3
The Tree
(Daniel 4)

Upon returning to his chambers after another delicious meal at the king's table that night, Daniel began to review the scroll he had left lying on the floor. The scroll was open to the only section that Daniel had not written himself. He had decided to include this bit of text at the direction of his God, but also in memory of his old friend, King Nebuchadnezzar.

The king had written a treatise about a spectacular event that had occurred to him early in Daniel's exile from Jerusalem. This extreme time of trouble that came upon the king had endeared him to Daniel. This new blossoming friendship had come because Daniel had chosen to befriend the king, staying by his side, protecting, feeding, and caring for him when everyone else had fled the scene. The king recognized Daniel's loyalty, and from this a unique and close relationship sprang up between the two.

Isn't that how good friendships often come to be? They happen when we are willing to give of ourselves to care for someone else. This is exactly what happened with Daniel on the day the king was caught, again, singing his own praises. But this time, God would not put up with it anymore. He had warned the king of his weakness in this area and had instructed him about how to humble himself rather than lift himself up. God had told the king that He wanted to bless him. But before He could do that, Nebuchadnezzar had to humble himself and recognize that only his Creator was worthy of his complete devotion.

Sadly, the king wouldn't listen and paid a huge price for his disobedience. For the next seven years the king lost his bearings and acted exactly like an animal, grazing on grass and sleeping out in the open. Only Daniel's companionship kept him from being utterly forgotten. But as the old prophet knew from the lessons he had learned at the hand of Elohim, trusting and relying on his Creator was always the best bet.

Sure enough, God came through and restored Nebuchadnezzar's rightful mind and his rightful place as king, but only because there was a job God intended for the king to do in the time he had been given on this earth. In the aftermath, the king's response of praise and worship was one of the reasons that Daniel included King Nebuchadnezzar's letter near the middle of his newly finished scroll. Rubbing his beard, the old prophet knew that very soon he would be reunited with his old friend in the world to come.

Daniel 4 is unique among biblical writings. It is the only chapter in the Bible that was written by a non-Hebrew. The person who wrote this was Nebuchadnezzar himself.

The statue studied in the previous chapter represents Satan's evil empires throughout the world. Satan is attempting to rule and reign over the entire world in place of the true God. And that's exactly what happens just before the end of the age at the second coming of Yeshua. Nebuchadnezzar is represented as the head, the pinnacle, of Satan's power and authority on earth. The text strongly implies that God is able to convert this very person that Satan has picked out to be the head of his seven evil kingdoms:

> "Now I, Nebuchadnezzar, praise, exalt, and honor the king of heaven, for all his works are true and his ways just, and he is able to humble those who walk in pride." (Daniel 4:37)

In addition, ancient tradition informs us that Daniel and Nebuchadnezzar had a very close relationship[1]. History is embellished to indicate that this closeness developed during the trial which came upon Nebuchadnezzar.

What's in a Name?

According to several Bible dictionaries and commentaries, Nebuchadnezzar was generally considered the greatest and most powerful of the Babylonian kings. His name literally meant "Prince of the god Nebu." Nebu was the Babylonian name for the false god that the Greeks called Mercury. The word *chadnez* meant "the god," while *zar* meant "prince." [2]

Belteshazzar, the Babylonian name given to Daniel, may have meant "Bel is the keeper of secrets."[3] Bel was a "chief god of the Babylonians, worshiped in the tower of Babel."[4] Gesenius proposes that Daniel's Babylonian name meant "Bel's prince, i.e. prince whom Bel favours."[5]

Chances are we'll have to ask Daniel himself when we meet him in the hereafter.

The Second Vision in Daniel

King Nebuchadnezzar had a vision of a huge tree in the midst of the earth, whose height was very great. It was large and strong and was visible to the ends of the whole earth. The tree provided cover and food for all the beasts of the field and the birds of the sky, and for all other living creatures.

Then an angel from heaven came and chopped the tree down, stripped off the foliage, and scattered the fruit. Immediately all the animals fled, but the stump was left in the ground and a band of iron and bronze was put around its base. In Daniel 4:2–3 we see the king responding after the fact to these terrifying events. His response was the way God wants us to respond when trouble enters our lives.

> [2] "It has seemed good to me to declare the signs and wonders
> which the Most High God has done for me.
> [3] How great are His signs
> And how mighty are His wonders!
> His kingdom is an everlasting kingdom
> And His dominion is from generation to generation."
> (Daniel 4:2–3)

In regard to these calamitous events, Nebuchadnezzar responds, "It seems good to declare the signs and wonders which the Most High God has done for me." Even though these events were terrible, Nebuchadnezzar realized that they were for his own good. And, in both of these verses he's praising God and giving Him glory for what He's allowed into his life.

How do we respond when trouble enters our lives? Do we thank God in the midst and praise Him in our prayers, even though we just lost our job or are having trouble with our spouse? Usually not. What we normally do is get angry with God and blame Him for our trouble, asking Him, "Why did you allow this to happen? I didn't deserve this! This goes against all of my plans. What good will come out of this?" We then end the whole thing by deciding not to talk to God for a period of days or weeks.

Yet here we see Nebuchadnezzar doing exactly the right thing. God punished him, and in the process Nebuchadnezzar's heart was revealed. He recognized that he was wrong and was going in the opposite direction, which God had warned him about. He turned to God, realizing that he needed to respond differently, then praised God in the midst of all his troubles, and afterward as well.

Nebuchadnezzar's Learning Curve

How many times do we learn from our own mistakes? Or, do we just keep going around in circles, making the same old mistakes and requiring God to punish us again and again? God loves us so much that He's not going to give up, and all of these chastisements are for our own good. Getting angry with God and deciding to ignore Him is exactly the worst response.

Recall that Joseph, one of the twelve sons of Israel, got sent to Egypt, was made a slave, and was then thrown into prison. This all happened after Joseph revealed the visions that he'd had to his family, in which they were all destined to bow down to him. Perhaps Joseph had the same problem – pride. And what happened? In Joseph's mind, God was revealing to him that he was going to be a ruler, but the circumstances that unfolded in the months after his dream made it look like he was going in exactly the opposite direction.

And so is the case in our own lives. Many times God gives us guidance and insight about our futures, but then it appears that the circumstances lead in an opposite direction. This is characteristic of how God often works in our lives. God wants us to acquire more maturity, or a special ability that we need to learn and develop, before we can actually take a position of honor and responsibility that would then allow us to learn even more.

Nebuchadnezzar had the same learning curve. God was willing to put him through a certain hell to teach him what he needed to realize. So, let's find out what this "hell" was.

Nebuchadnezzar's Vision

It seems that what God was revealing to Nebuchadnezzar was the current condition of his kingdom, which had ruled over a world where all men and women were protected and fed by the power and productivity of that kingdom. But it would all come to an end for Nebuchadnezzar at least, for the tree that represented the king was about to take a fall.

The description of what happens to the king starts in verse 14.

> [13] 'I was looking in the visions in my mind as I lay on my bed, and behold, an angelic watcher, a holy one, descended from heaven.
> [14] He shouted out and spoke as follows:
> "Chop down the tree and cut off its branches,

Strip off its foliage and scatter its fruit;
Let the beasts flee from under it
And the birds from its branches.
[15] Yet leave the stump with its roots in the ground,
But with a band of iron and bronze around it
In the new grass of the field;
And let him be drenched with the dew of heaven,
And let him share with the beasts in the grass of the earth.
[16] Let his mind be changed from that of a man
And let a beast's mind be given to him,
And let seven periods of time pass over him.'"
(Daniel 4:13–16)

This whole vision started with the proclamation of an angelic watcher in verse 13. The Hebrew word here is *iyr* which means "a guard, a watcher, a name of angels in the later Hebrew, from their guarding the souls of men."[6] Angels are the guardians of men's souls. This description is usually applied to teraphim, one of the three types of angels encountered in the Bible and in other ancient Jewish writings. Cherubim are the angels surrounding the throne of God, and seraphim are known as the angels of fire, whose primary job is to deliver messages.

On the other hand, teraphim are the ones that ride on your bumper. We all have angels that guard over us. These are the ones that Paul writes about when he instructs us to be hospitable: "Do not neglect to show hospitality to strangers, for by this some have entertained angels without knowing it" (Hebrews 13:2).

Such angels can appear "as men." This particular angel, appearing to Nebuchadnezzar, shouted out instructions to chop down the tree (verse 14, above) and cut off its branches. The obvious implication is that the king was going to lose his position of authority, and in verse 16 we find that something very untoward happens to him.

One of the more literal translations of the Bible, the NASB, states Daniel 4:16 as "Let his mind be changed from that of a man and let a beast's mind be given to him." The word "mind" here is the Aramaic word *levav*, which means "heart, mind"[7] and essentially refers to a person's soul, emotions, intellect, and wisdom. Levav is a common Hebrew word used in the biblical text and usually gets interpreted "heart."

Unfortunately, a misunderstanding arises between the Aramaic and the Hebrew meaning and the English concept lying behind the word "heart." For example, Psalm 62:8 says:

> Trust in Him at all times, O people;
> Pour out your heart before Him;
> God is a refuge for us.

Here *levav* gets translated as it normally does, as "heart." The English gives the idea that we're pouring out emotion before God. We thus have images in our minds of weeping and crying, but that's not at all what the Hebrew in this verse is saying. What it is suggesting is that with your mind you should pour out concentrated, well thought-out expressions of your need for Him. Psalm 90:12 includes the same idea:

> So teach us to number our days,
> That we may present to You a heart of wisdom.

A better translation for the word "heart" in this verse would be that God wants us to present a *mind* of wisdom. In Hebrew, the concept of the heart is tied together with the concept of wisdom. So a sound heart is equal to a wise, well-trained mind. In Hebrew thinking, our emotions should be kept under control and should follow what the mind has decided to do through wisdom. Man's actions should not be governed by emotion, leaving the mind (or the intelligence) of a person to be dragged along for the ride.

The Hebrew concept of this heart/mind understanding is also primarily associated with the concept in Hebrew of the soul. Therefore, what Daniel 4:16 is really conveying is that the emotion and the mind of Nebuchadnezzar, which was equal to the soul of the man, was going to be removed and replaced by the mind, instincts, and appetites of a beast.

Why Are We Saved By the Blood?

Recall that Daniel 4 was originally written in Aramaic. The Aramaic word *levav*, translated as *mind* or *heart*, can also mean *soul*. The Hebrew word for soul, *nephesh*, would most likely have been used if Daniel 4:16 was written in Hebrew rather than Aramaic. The first time nephesh appears is in Genesis 1:20:

> Then God said, "Let the waters teem with swarms of living creatures, and let birds fly above the earth in the open expanse of the heavens."

The underlying Hebrew word for creatures is nephesh. This verse teaches us that God created all kinds of living creatures that He said were the equivalent of living souls. Unfortunately, Genesis 2:7 gets translated as:

> Then the Lord God formed man of dust from the ground, and breathed into his nostrils the breath of life; and man became a living being.

The translators, in describing the creation of man, called him a "living being" for the same word, nephesh. What the reader loses by this inconsistency in translation is that God is explaining that both animal life and human life have a soul, a nephesh.

The difference is that mankind was made by hands molding his very form and came to life with a much more intimate breath from the mouth of God. This is in contrast to how God spoke the animal kingdom into being.

Now let's take the concept of nephesh one step further. Leviticus 17:11 says:

> For the life [*nephesh*] of the flesh is in the blood, and I have given it to you on the altar to make atonement for your souls; for it is the blood by reason of the life [*nephesh*] that makes atonement.

In the verse above, the Hebrew word "nephesh" gets interpreted as "life" twice. By understanding that nephesh means "soul," this verse is communicating a very interesting concept. We think that it's the blood of Yeshua, or Jesus, that was shed on the cross that pays the price for our sins. But this verse is explaining that it's the soul, or the nephesh, that's contained IN the blood that actually makes the atonement.

In other words, He's offering up his soul to make atonement, knowing full well that the soul also embodies His earthly life.

Therefore, to summarize all this, the text of Daniel 4 is communicating to us that Nebuchadnezzar's nature – the very ways in which he thought, reasoned, and acted – was removed and replaced by the thought, reasoning, and actions of an animal.

So, when his wife called him a beast, she was right!

Banded by Brass

Nebuchadnezzar revealed to Daniel that the tree in his vision that was destined to be chopped down (and which represented Nebuchadnezzar himself) would have its stump left standing, capped with bands of iron and brass (bronze). In Hebrew, iron can represent angelic activity in the heavens or in the atmosphere, and brass can represent angelic activity on the earth. What these metallic symbols could therefore be representing (i.e., telling Nebuchadnezzar) is that God would be sending angels to protect the foundation of His kingdom while Nebuchadnezzar was going through this testing.

The word "brass" in Hebrew is *nekhoshet* and contains the Hebrew word for "serpent," *nakhash*. It is first used in Genesis 3 to describe the snake that Satan took the form of to tempt Eve. It also means to hiss, to whisper, or to practice divination. Therefore, what God could also be telling us here, by using the symbols of brass and iron around the stump that represents the king and his kingdom, is that, for a time, God will allow fallen angels (i.e., devils) to put Nebuchadnezzar under bondage.

This is exactly what God has done throughout the ages when dealing with and training mankind. God allows us to be tested, and we can lose authority and effectiveness. But it all has a purpose, and it's only for a time. For Nebuchadnezzar, this time was to last for seven years.

It is also interesting to note that brass is the metal of the third kingdom in the previous dream that King Nebuchadnezzar had about the statue made out of different metals. The third kingdom is represented as a mixture of metals, which is what bronze actually is. Likewise, the third kingdom was a mixture of the Medes and the Persians.

This idea of a tree representing a man or mankind is a common metaphor found in the Bible. References include Psalms 1:3, Isaiah 56:3, Jeremiah 17:8, and Matthew 7:17. Both kingdoms, the kingdom of God and the kingdom of Satan, are pictured, or metaphorically referenced, as trees. Certainly Satan's kingdom, right here in Daniel 4, is being depicted as a tree. And he is the head of the statue of the previous dream, which we have learned is a reference to the evil kingdoms that Satan has and is going to try to use to rule the whole world.

But also, God's kingdom is depicted by trees. Think of the Garden of Eden. God uses the tree of life to provide life and food and protection as did the tree in Nebuchadnezzar's vision. The tree of life was in the midst of the garden and provided for mankind's needs. God's kingdom meets man's needs through love, creating an environment of freedom so man can choose and prioritize His maker.

Conversely, Satan's kingdoms have been used to control mankind and put people under bondage. Today we see this phenomenon spreading throughout the world. The ideas of socialism are very well received, but they are actually a perversion of what God intends. Never does God promote the idea of forcing someone to meet the needs of others, especially when the recipients aren't attempting to meet their own needs.

Unfortunately, the United States is walking down that same road. In the effort to meet people's needs we are becoming a democracy instead of a republic. A democracy is not what our founding fathers created. In a democracy, the majority rules the minority. When the majority of people in America are the recipients of other people's hard-earned assets and rights, the majority will rule and will dictate ever more rigid terms, whereas a republic's primary purpose is to protect the rights and properties of the minority against the majority. Satan will find a very receptive political environment in the days ahead if we continue down this road.

In Daniel 4:30, we find the king doing exactly what many people do – taking pride for their achievements while not recognizing all along who provided the talents, the increase, and the blessings. As did the king, we Americans tend to take pride in our achievements as well, ignoring the fact that God was the source. This was the reason God tested the king. God realizes that in order for mankind to appreciate Him, He must remove pride. Because of pride we get tested.

Hebrew is a unique language in that each of the 22 consonants not only makes a sound but is also a picture which conveys a meaning. The Hebrew word for lifting up or exalting oneself is *room*. The pictography of the Hebrew letters in this word says that "pride is the man who covenants with or attaches himself to chaos." So, if you want more chaos in your life, continue to walk in pride.

Pictographs: Each Letter Is a Picture

Every letter in the Hebrew alphabet is a picture, and the letter used to look like the picture. The shapes of the letters have changed over the years so sometimes it's hard to see the picture in the letter – but the meaning behind the picture for each letter still functions. Hebrew is unique in that not only are the letters phonetic, but words are formed from picture-letters which have meaning.

Therefore the meaning of a Hebrew word can be deciphered by stringing together the individual meanings of its letters. It is

---

astounding to think that a language can have within the very letters which form the words a key to understanding their meaning. Here is an example from a word you are undoubtedly familiar with: *shalom.* The Hebrew letters which make up "shalom" convey this meaning: destroy the authority that binds you to chaos. In other words, God's idea of peace (shalom) is getting rid of the chaotic things which we allow to control us.

Another example is the word "Satan" which is the same word in Hebrew as it is in English. The pictograph for Satan (the meaning of the letters strung together) is "a snake that devours life." Could there be a better definition of Satan?

One of the most powerful pictographs is the word "Torah." These letters show God's very purpose for His Word: to reveal the man nailed to the cross.

A Kingdom Without Pride

God's kingdom, in contrast, operates completely differently, and so should we. The verses below instruct us against pride and ask us to walk in humility, putting other people's interests before our own:

> ³Do nothing from selfishness or empty conceit, but with humility of mind regard one another as more important than yourselves; ⁴ do not merely look out for your own personal interests, but also for the interests of others. (Philippians 2:3–4)

You might ask yourself, "Why does God hate pride so much?" The answer is found in Isaiah 14:13–14, below. This passage describes Satan, who is walking in pride. He is proclaiming that in his heart he will ascend to God's throne and make himself like the Most High.

> ¹³"But you said in your heart,
> 'I will ascend to heaven;
> I will raise my throne above the stars of God,

> And I will sit on the mount of assembly
> In the recesses of the north.
> [14] I will ascend above the heights of the clouds;
> I will make myself like the Most High.'"

The point is that if you're going to be used by God He will also put you through some hard times. The purpose will be to deal with your shortcomings of character. We can respond in various ways to God's correction. We can buck His instructions, we can blame Him, we can get mad at Him, we can tell Him that He's not doing a very good job. We can decide that we're miserable failures and fall into a deep depression. We can then tell God that we don't like the way He's running things or that we really don't deserve all of these disasters.

Or, we can do the right thing, which is to stand fast and thank God for the testings that bring forth the character qualities we need to develop to properly manage the authority that He wants to give us. Remember, there is nothing greater than our ability to resist:

> No temptation has overtaken you but such as is common to man; and God is faithful, who will not allow you to be tempted beyond what you are able, but with the temptation will provide the way of escape also, so that you will be able to endure it. (I Corinthians 10:13)

There is an interesting parallel between Nebuchadnezzar's kingdom and his tests, represented by the huge tree and the giant statue in the previous dream. Recall that the statue represents the kingdoms of the beast, the false messiah, and Nebuchadnezzar is its head. In both of these visions the foundation of these kingdoms is pride. Both kingdoms are called Babylon. Both the beast and the king have their natures changed. Both build images and demand that the people worship them (Revelation 13:14-15).

Both kingdoms are then cut down. Both kingdoms are given seven years. Sanity, humility, and righteousness returned to the king after seven years, after he realized that God rules in the affairs of man. The false messiah's (antichrist's) kingdom will last seven years, after which sanity and humility will return to the earth by the setting up of God's reign.

As Nebuchadnezzar finished writing this chapter, he expressed an attitude that should be found in all of us as we go through trouble and tribulation:

> "Now I, Nebuchadnezzar, praise, exalt and honor the King of heaven, for all His works are true and His ways just, and He is able to humble those who walk in pride." (Daniel 4:37)

4
The Handwriting on the Wall
(Daniel 5)

Startled, the old prophet woke up. In contrast to the peace he had felt the night before, his dreams and old memories made him unsettled. Satan loved to throw circumstances at him that would get his attention off his Maker and onto seemingly impossible disasters. At least they appeared to be impossible . . . but not to God.

It took all the faith Daniel could muster to restore that peace once it was lost, for it was almost always replaced by an uneasy feeling that would steal away his confidence and destroy his self-worth. It was not the circumstances surrounding him but the power of the evil one that attempted to destroy his reliance on God Himself.

Case in point was his most recent dream, which reminded him of King Belshazzar. This vision not only had negative ramifications for Daniel but also against Belshazzar, the grandson of his friend, King Nebuchadnezzar. Belshazzar now ruled Babylon but had no peace, personally or otherwise, because he had no heart for God. What was about to happen to him would end his reign in calamity.

Daniel was sure that Belshazzar had begun giving his attention to other spiritual beings, those that Daniel called devils and demons. These unseen fallen angels had so distracted the king from the truth that he

commonly engaged in the most destructive behaviors. A lifestyle contrary in every way with~~was~~ *what* right was now guiding the king toward his
own destruction. And unfortunately, his own deception was causing
others to fall away as well.

It all came to a head when the king took his disobedience one step too
far. Belshazzar had decided to throw another of his grand parties, but
this time using the holy accouterments of the temple in Jerusalem. His
grandfather, King Nebuchadnezzar, had brought them back from Israel
after conquering Jerusalem and the surrounding land decades before.

As Daniel learned shortly thereafter, a hand appeared on the wall in the
banquet hall and wrote a message to the king himself. Daniel was called
in to interpret the message, for no one else could decipher the meaning.

The message was not good news. God had informed Belshazzar that his
reign was over. Specifically, God told him that he had been weighed
and been found wanting. In other words, the king's obedience to the
laws of God was too little and much too late.

That very night the armies of the Medes and the Persians dammed up
the Euphrates River that flowed under the outer wall and through the
city of Babylon. This allowed the conquering armies to march right
through the hole in the wall where the river had flowed into the city.
And that night, as the writing from God forewarned, the king was
destroyed and his kingdom was conquered.

Daniel recalled how he had run in fear of the events that he realized
were about to fall on the city. His friends, the authority he had earned
– indeed, his whole life – was now in danger from the fulfillment of
Belshazzar's word from God. Talk about being in the wrong place at
the wrong time! That was certainly enough to take away one's peace.

As God Himself made clear much later in Romans 8:28, everything
works together for good to those who love the Lord. In many ways the
conquest of Babylon was a non-event. Some of the people who lived
there didn't even know that they were under the rule of a new empire
until the next day. Mostly it all came down to the replacement of Baby-

lon's King Belshazzar with Darius, the new governor put in that position by Cyrus, king of the Medo-Persians. Daniel was soon elevated to a very high position within the Medo-Persian kingdom.

Now, Daniel arose to start the new day. As always he began with a conversation with his Maker.

Daniel 5 introduces us to King Belshazzar who was one of Nebuchadnezzar's grandsons. Ironically, for many centuries King Belshazzar's father, King Nabonidus, was the only king recorded in ancient documents who lived during the time of the Babylonian fall. His son was thought by leading scholars to be a complete fabrication by the writer of the book of Daniel. These so-called scholars, in their efforts to promote their belief that the book of Daniel was written near the first century BC, used the lack of Belshazzar's name in ancient records to prove their point.

However, as is so often the case, a huge library of tablets was found in the mid-19th century that made mention of Belshazzar, who ruled simultaneously with his father. It seems that King Nabonidus was, in fact, the last king to rule over Babylon, just before the Medo-Persians conquered the Babylonian Empire in 539 BC. But, because he was not popular with his people or with the religious leaders of his day, he tended to spend most of his time down in northern Arabia, which was part of his kingdom. He left his son, Belshazzar, to rule on a daily basis in his stead. This is why, when Daniel interprets the writing on the wall (which we'll learn about later), King Belshazzar was able to offer Daniel the third position in the kingdom, behind his father and himself (Daniel 5:16).

The Finger of God Points Out Pride

Recall the statue of the four different metals introduced in Daniel 2. We learned that the head of gold represented Babylon, while the next section, the arms and chest, represented the Medo-Persian Empire.

Daniel 5 deals with the events surrounding the final days of the Babylonian Empire before they were overthrown by the Medo-Persians.

> [17]Then Daniel answered and said before the king, "Keep your gifts for yourself or give your rewards to someone else; however, I will read the inscription to the king and make the interpretation known to him. [18] O king, the Most High God granted sovereignty, grandeur, glory and majesty to Nebuchadnezzar your father. [19] Because of the grandeur which He bestowed on him, all the peoples, nations and men of every language feared and trembled before him; whomever he wished he killed and whomever he wished he spared alive; and whomever he wished he elevated and whomever he wished he humbled.
>
> [20] "But when his heart was lifted up and his spirit became so proud that he behaved arrogantly, he was deposed from his royal throne and his glory was taken away from him. [21] He was also driven away from mankind, and his heart was made like that of beasts, and his dwelling place was with the wild donkeys. He was given grass to eat like cattle, and his body was drenched with the dew of heaven until he recognized that the Most High God is ruler over the realm of mankind and that He sets over it whomever He wishes.
>
> [22] "Yet you, his son, Belshazzar, have not humbled your heart, even though you knew all this, [23] but you have exalted yourself against the Lord of heaven; and they have brought the vessels of His house before you, and you and your nobles, your wives and your concubines have been drinking wine from them; and you have praised the gods of silver and gold, of bronze, iron, wood and stone, which do not see, hear or understand. But the God in whose hand are your life-breath and all your ways, you have not glorified." (Daniel 5:17–23)

Note that verse 18 in the biblical text above refers to Nebuchadnezzar as Belshazzar's "father," although Belshazzar's actual father was clearly

Nabonidus. Nabonidus' own father was Nebuchadnezzar, made clear via ancient records that have been discovered within the last two hundred years.[1]

Most modern biblical translations use the word "grandfather" in no more than two or three versions, but that was the true relationship between Nebuchadnezzar and Belshazzar. This confusion is made possible because the Hebrew word for father can mean "grandfather" or even "ancestor."[2]

King Belshazzar was a proud man. In the text above, God goes right to the root of the king's problem. He did not learn from experience – or, in this case, from his grandfather's experience. Daniel specifically tells him, in verse 22, that he has not humbled his heart even though he knew all the trouble that his grandfather went through when confronted by God due to his pride. Recall that King Nebuchadnezzar was changed by God into an animal for seven years, after which he completely turned away from his pride and recognized the true God.

Nebuchadnezzar's grandson, while throwing another of his many parties for all the leading families in Babylon, decided to take the temple implements that Nebuchadnezzar had stolen from the temple in Jerusalem some 70 years earlier when he conquered that land. And, King Belshazzar decided to drink from them during his party, representing disrespect and a major slap in the face to the real God.

In verse 4 we are told that in the process of drinking the wine from these temple goblets, the king and his compatriats praised the gods of gold, silver, bronze, iron, wood, and stone. God uses this description repeataedly when relating Satan's efforts to rule the earth. Certainly, in Daniel 2, these same metals are used in the construction of that huge statue that represented these ancient evil empires.

Also, in the following verse from Revelation we find the same metals and materials describing the gods of this world, Satan and his devils:

> The rest of mankind, who were not killed by these plagues, did not repent of the works of their hands, so as not to

worship demons, and the idols of gold and of silver and of brass and of stone and of wood, which can neither see nor hear nor walk. (Revelation 9:20)

Even at the end of the age, just before the second coming of the Messiah, we see the world falling down and worshipping these same so-called gods. And this occurs after they've gone through hellacious tribulation, poured out by God to get their attention and give them one last chance to recognize Him as the true God.

The REAL Handwriting on the Wall

The next segment of Daniel 5 tells us the story of the handwriting on the wall:

> [24] "Then the hand was sent from Him and this inscription was written out. [25] Now this is the inscription that was written out: 'MENĒ, MENĒ, TEKĒL, UPHARSIN.'

> [26] "This is the interpretation of the message: 'MENĒ—God has numbered your kingdom and put an end to it. [27] 'TEKĒL'—you have been weighed on the scales and found deficient. [28] 'PERĒS'—your kingdom has been divided and given over to the Medes and Persians."

> [29] Then Belshazzar gave orders, and they clothed Daniel with purple and put a necklace of gold around his neck, and issued a proclamation concerning him that he now had authority as the third ruler in the kingdom.

> [30] That same night Belshazzar the Chaldean king was slain. [31] So Darius the Mede received the kingdom at about the age of sixty-two. (Daniel 5:24–31)

The definition of the Hebrew/Aramaic words written on the wall is:

- *Mene* = numbered.
- *Tekel* = weighed (this word is used to physically weigh things on a scale).
- *Peres* = divided.

God was telling Belshazzar that he had been counted, weighed, and found to be wanting, as in "he is too light for the appropriate weight of the measure." To be too light means to be lacking the substance and character that God values. Because of this, Belshazzar's kingdom would now be divided.

It seems that many people today share these same shortcomings. Whether they are found in the non-believing world or in the church world, lots of folks can be described as being "too light for God's taste." Many people are lacking in substance and character, especially the substance that can recognize truth clearly without being blown around by every wind of doctrine.

Some people pride themselves today as certainly being "characters" indeed, but that's hardly the character that God is calling us to have. Are we stable, reliable, dependable, full of wisdom, and able to prioritize other people's needs over our own? These are the qualities Daniel had, but certainly not Belshazzar. Which best describes you?

Why Was Translating the Handwriting So Difficult?

There is much speculation on why the king's wise men couldn't translate the writing on the wall, as written by the finger of God. Certainly they were well-versed in the Hebrew language and could have interpreted the message if it had been written in Hebrew or any of the other languages that were written or spoken in the lands that were controlled by the king.

There is some speculation that the message written on Belshazzar's wall was encrypted. From ancient times, the Jewish scribes had devised two types of encryption techniques that were known only to them – *album* and *atbash*.

In *album*, the first encryption technique, the second half of the Hebrew alephbet was overlaid over the first half. So, *aleph* would then become a *lamed* and *kaf* would become a *tav*. This encryption technique was also used in Isaiah 7:6.[3]

In *atbash*, the second encryption technique, the second half of the Hebrew alephbet would again be overlaid over the first half, but this time *backwards*. So, the *aleph* would then be a *tav* and the *kaf* would be a *lamed*. This encryption technique was used in Jeremiah 25:26, 51:41 and 51:1.[4]

Again, this is just speculation, but the above offers one good reason why none of the other scholars were able to interpret the words written on the wall. The writing itself was "mene, mene, tekel, peres."

The Fall of Babylon

From ancient historical records we know that on October 12th of 536 BC, while the party and the confrontation between Belshazzar and God was occuring, Cyrus, the king of the Medo-Persians, was outside the very walls of Babylon, diverting the Euphrates River that used to run through the city. The Babylonians had built the wall surrounding the city in such a manner that allowed the river to go underneath the wall, through the city, and exit under the city wall on the other side. By diverting the river, King Cyrus created a pathway for his army to march underneath the walls exactly where the river used to flow.

King Cyrus was known as a very brave warrior, but a very tolerant leader as well. His mother was a Mede but his father was a Persian. These two people groups originated from what would be known today as the eastern and the northern portions of Iran and beyond.

[27] "It is I who says to the depth of the sea, 'Be dried up!'
And I will make your rivers dry.
[28] It is I who says of Cyrus, 'He is My shepherd!'
And he will perform all My desire.'
And he declares of Jerusalem, 'She will be built,'
And of the temple, 'Your foundation will be laid.'" (Isaiah 44:27–28)

[1]Thus says the LORD to Cyrus His anointed,
Whom I have taken by the right hand,
To subdue nations before him
And to loose the loins of kings;
To open doors before him so that gates will not be shut:
[2]"I will go before you and make the rough places smooth;
I will shatter the doors of bronze and cut through their iron bars.
[3]I will give you the treasures of darkness
And hidden wealth of secret places,
So that you may know that it is I,
The LORD, the God of Israel, who calls you by your name.
[4]For the sake of Jacob My servant,
And Israel My chosen one,
I have also called you by your name;
I have given you a title of honor
Though you have not known Me.
[5]I am the LORD, and there is no other;
Besides Me there is no God.
I will gird you, though you have not known Me." (Isaiah 45:1–5)

Sometime after the fall of the city to King Cyrus, the prophet Daniel presented to the new king the ancient scroll of Isaiah. The prophet Isaiah lived 150 to 250 years before the fall of Babylon. His primary mission was to prophesy about future events that would affect his people, Israel. The prophecy above actually describes the fall of Babylon and refers to the king of the Medo-Persians by name many years before he was born.

In modern times we Bible believers think of King Cyrus as a pretty bad dude. But here, in the passage above, God calls Cyrus his anointed and prophesies that Cyrus will be God's shepherd. Cyrus will allow Jerusalem to be rebuilt, and the temple's foundations will be laid by the king's proclamation.

After seeing his name in print on scrolls written long before his birth, Cyrus probably became positively inclined toward the Jews. In fact, soon thereafter he released the Jews to go home. He financed their trip, gave them back their temple implements, and gave additional donations for the rebuilding of the temple.

I believe Daniel 5 is inserted into the Bible to serve as a warning. Belshazzar completely ignored the lessons that he should have learned from his father's experience. Why are we so dense? Is it because we have become so taken up with ourselves? Do we focus on the pleasures of this world rather than the kingdom of God? Do we sometimes let the cares of this world, such as our jobs, relationships, and other problems, distract us? Do we suffer from delusions of grandeur about ourselves?

The lesson for us is that we always need to keep our focus and our attention on God, by taking Him with us during our days wherever we go. And, by being conscious of His presence and majesty in our lives.

5

The Four Beasts
(Daniel 6-7)

The next day, as Daniel was picking up some fresh fruit at the street market in Babylon in the midst of a huge crowd, he observed an animal circus setting up for its first show. It had just arrived and everyone wanted to watch the arenas being set up. But mostly, they wanted to watch the unloading of all the animals. Daniel enjoyed it too. He loved to be wowed by the diversity and creativity that his God had put into His creations. To Daniel it revealed the awesome intelligence and wisdom Elohim possessed.

Then the lions appeared. And yes, they were stately, proud, and masters of their own world. But lions had another effect on Daniel. Every time he saw them they brought terrible memories of persecution. It all started when Darius appointed Daniel over the 120 princes who governed the whole kingdom. It seemed that many of the qualities that God had nurtured in him over the years now became obvious to the new king. Even Daniel himself could recognize the increase of maturity in his life. But the more he grew, the more humble he became.

Even so, not everyone appreciated Daniel. There was lust for the great power that had been bestowed on him, and there were attempts on his life. This should have been the crowning point in his life, a celebration of the fact that he was now in his eighties and had been in service to

75

kings for most of his life. But you can never let your guard down when your enemy is the kingdom of darkness. Jealousy is a mighty force, and that is what the powers of darkness used to try to end Daniel's life.

That's where the lions come in. Certain politicians, with a lust for power, passed a law that no one could petition any "god" except the king for thirty days. Daniel knew about this new law but prayed to the true God anyway. Unfortunately, he was caught in the act.

Daniel's punishment for this "crime" was to be thrown to the lions. He remembered well the fear, the smells, and the hungry looks on the faces of those beasts as he sat alone in their den. But he had learned that God expected him to be both a testimony and an inspiration for others. So, as he sat there in that cave, filled with the stench of the beasts, peace once again entered his soul as he prayed to his Protector. This same peace had come over his three friends too, as they were thrown into a fiery furnace. God had come through for them and He would come through for Daniel now.

That is exactly what happened. After Daniel spent all night trying not to look very tasty, his good friend the king, who had been tricked into passing this murderous law, came to Daniel's rescue. When the first light of day showed that Daniel was still alive, Darius reversed the situation by saving him and throwing the perpetrators into the lion's den instead.

What happened next was shocking. Before the guilty parties could even reach the ground, the lions snatched them from the air and devoured them on the spot. Walking home, Daniel had to work hard to get that terrifying scene out of his mind. It still lived there in all of its gore and screams and colors.

Daniel knew that the key to removing bad memories was forgiveness. That he had done long ago. But the other dilemma he still had trouble with — stopping the terrifying memories from playing over and over in his mind, reinforcing the emotions and the violations each time. Seeing the circus lions seemed to trigger those old thoughts he so much wanted to forget.

Daniel was determined to shut off replaying those ugly memories as surely as God had shut those lions' mouths.

As we highlighted earlier, the book of Daniel contains seven dreams or visions – seven revelations from God. In the Bible's typical Hebraic fashion, the first revelation, the four-metal statue, gave us an overview of the seven evil kingdoms of this world that would rule from before Daniel's time and after, until the coming of God and the setting up of His kingdom. God's kingdom would be the eighth kingdom. The number eight, in the Bible, represents the concept of renewal, or new beginnings. And that certainly will be the case, since the previous seven kingdoms have been empowered and run by Satan.

On that basis alone, God's kingdom will represent a new beginning. Meanwhile, we are discovering that the next six visions in the book of Daniel expound on one or more of the final kingdoms that will attempt to rule the world via the authority of Satan.

Daniel's vision in chapter 7 is the fourth of these revelations and focuses on four beasts that will come. These beasts depict the four sections of the statue made of metals from Daniel 2, the four kingdoms that would come from Daniel's time on. In essence, God is giving us a whole additional layer of information regarding these same four evil empires.

> [1] In the first year of Belshazzar king of Babylon Daniel saw a dream and visions in his mind as he lay on his bed; then he wrote the dream down and related the following summary of it. [2] Daniel said, "I was looking in my vision by night, and behold, the four winds of heaven were stirring up the great sea. [3] And four great beasts were coming up from the sea, different from one another. [4] The first was like a lion and had the wings of an eagle. I kept looking until its wings were plucked, and it was lifted up from the ground and made to stand on two feet like a man; a human mind also was given to it.

⁵ "And behold, another beast, a second one, resembling a bear. And it was raised up on one side, and three ribs were in its mouth between its teeth; and thus they said to it, 'Arise, devour much meat!'

⁶ "After this I kept looking, and behold, another one, like a leopard, which had on its back four wings of a bird; the beast also had four heads, and dominion was given to it.

⁷ "After this I kept looking in the night visions, and behold, a fourth beast, dreadful and terrifying and extremely strong; and it had large iron teeth. It devoured and crushed and trampled down the remainder with its feet; and it was different from all the beasts that were before it, and it had ten horns. ⁸ While I was contemplating the horns, behold, another horn, a little one, came up among them, and three of the first horns were pulled out by the roots before it; and behold, this horn possessed eyes like the eyes of a man and a mouth uttering great boasts." (Daniel 7:1–8)

Daniel was about 67 years old when he had this dream, and it occurred in the first year of the reign of Nebuchadnezzar's grandson, Belshazzar. In this vision Daniel observes four beasts: a lion, a bear, a leopard, and a ten-horned, iron-toothed monster that doesn't correlate – in Daniel's mind anyway – with any known beasts. Most of Daniel's remaining visions will focus on this last beast.

The First Beast

We are told that the first beast, the lion, represents the kingdom of Babylon. It has eagle wings and a man's heart. In excavating the ancient city of Babylon, the archeologists discovered that on its gates were lions with eagle's wings. Recall that this kingdom, here being represented as a lion, was the head of gold of that great statue in Nebuchadnezzar's dream, which Daniel interpreted.

Descriptions of this kingdom in Daniel 7:4 say that a man's heart was given to it. This could be an allusion to Nebuchadnezzar being given a new heart after his confrontation with God and overcoming the pride that he once had. Recall that his human soul was replaced by an animal soul for seven years. Then, after Nebuchadnezzar humbled himself, God restored his heart and his identity as a person.

Recall, also, that his hair grew and covered him like eagle's feathers, and his nails grew out like eagle's claws. But he was allowed to stand, once again, like a man. His heart and mind were restored, which in Hebrew represent his *nephesh,* or soul. In other words, this lion beast was given back his original soul.

We haven't gotten to the fourth beast in Daniel's vision yet, but it should be emphasized that the first three beasts all contain attributes of the fourth beast. In other words, the fourth beast is a composite being of the previous three. That's one of the reasons why Daniel is not given a "created" animal to compare it with.

The Hebrew words that get interpreted as "evil beast" are usually associated with what the Bible calls Nephilim. The first time the word Nephilim appears in the Bible, in Genesis 6, it often gets interpreted as "giants." The *im* on the end of Nephilim makes it plural; Nephal would be the singular. These evil beings, during Noah's day, were the result of physical unions between angelic beings and human women. Indeed, this is one of the major reasons why God brought on the Flood, to expunge these malevolent creatures from the earth.

The kingdom that Daniel is prophesying about existed in the sixth century BC, long after the Flood occurred and exterminated the Nephilim. But here we see that Daniel 7 could be alluding to these evil beings once again re-emerging onto the face of the earth. Genesis 6 actually warns us that this would be the case, for it says that these beings existed before the Flood, but also afterwards:

> The Nephilim were on the earth in those days, *and also afterward*, when the sons of God came in to the daughters of men, and they bore children by them. (Genesis 6:4) [Italics added]

All of the kingdoms have been tyrannical and evil, perpetrating crimes against mankind and especially against Israel. But the evil of the last evil kingdom, the seventh, will be beyond imagination. But so will God's response. His final response will mirror His initial reaction to these satanically created men-beasts called Nephilim – the Flood that destroyed the entire creation at the time. Fire will be included in God's last response to once and for all, deal with this perverted rebellion against His creation.

The fourth beast, representing the final kingdom on the face of the earth prior to the coming of God, is a composite of the previous three beasts. Therefore, what Daniel 7:19–27 is implying is that also, during the end days, these Nephilim will re-emerge. This idea is further supported by Revelation 9:1-3. The locusts that are released during the last of days from the pit in this passage are allusions to these fallen angels that were locked away millennia ago for their perverted sexual crimes against women back before the Flood. They will once again be released on mankind to do the very same thing.

The Second Beast

Following the lion that appeared to Daniel in his dream came a bear with three ribs between its teeth. It was told to arise and devour much flesh. In contrast to lions, which are extremely agile and quick (and which perfectly describes Babylon in its prime), bears are more plodding and ponderous. But at the same time they can be very powerful predators. This portrays the next world-ruling kingdom, the Medo-Persians.

Xerxes was known to be a very intelligent leader and was in charge of a 2.5 million-man army which conquered the known world. However, his army was much like the bear – very powerful but slow and ponderous. The Persian Empire had three major conquests during its prime, which are represented by the three ribs. The first was Lydia, in Turkey. This battle occurred in western Turkey in 547 BC, near the shores of the Aegean Sea.

Cyrus was the commander at the time. Just eight years later, in 539 BC, he conquered Babylon as well. This was the second rib, or the second conquest.

In 525 BC, Cambyses led the Persian army in their conquest of Egypt. The bear was told to rise up and consume much flesh, and this kingdom's prey did consume much flesh in the form of the human lives that it destroyed. As Adam said in Genesis 2:23, "This is now bone of my bones, and flesh of my flesh." The same words for bones (rib) and flesh are what the bear was told to consume.

The Third Beast

Alexander the Great, who led the Greek Empire in the latter part of the fourth century BC, represents the third beast, which is a leopard. This leopard is described in Daniel 7:6 as having four wings like those of a bird on its back. It also had four heads, and great authority and dominion was given to it.

Leopards are known as one of the fastest predators on earth. This attribute perfectly described Alexander the Great and the Greek Empire, for in ten years Alexander was able to conquer Egypt all the way north to the Black Sea, and from Greece all the way east to India.

Whereas most fathers allow their sons to inherit their kingdoms, Alexander the Great bequeathed his kingdom to the "strong." This basically set up a fight between his top four generals, who wound up splitting the land into four separate kingdoms with each general ruling his own.

These four kingdoms and their commanders were:

- Cassander, who took Greece and Macedonia.
- Lysimachus, who took Turkey.
- Seleucus, who formed the Seleucid Empire. Today that would encompass Syria, Iran, and lands farther east.
- Ptolemy, who ruled over the lands to the south, including Egypt.

In the ensuing prophecies in Daniel, the Seleucid and Ptolemic Empires become the dominant players. They battled with each other again and again. Decades later the Seleucid Empire was ruled by Antiochus Epiphanes who, we will learn, becomes a type of false messiah.

This third beast, the leopard, is seen with four wings and four heads. In addition to being quick, leopards are also reclusive. You don't see them. They blend in with the background. This characteristic is very similar to the Greek Empire. It was quick and came out of nowhere.

The word "four" in the passage describing this leopard is the Hebrew word *arba*. In addition to meaning four it also means "giant ones," as in "ones from the tribe of the Anakim."[1] The Anakim are referred to many times in the Old Testament, especially in Joshua, as one of the tribes of Canaan. They are described as people who were giants. These are some of the ones that God wanted the Israelites to completely eliminate, and the reason now becomes clear. They were Nephilim, not humans. This exonerates God from the oft-slung criticisms that He was unmerciful and ruthless in telling the Israelites to wipe out the Canaanites when they entered the land. Nephilim are unredeemable and extremely dangerous.

The Fourth Beast

The three beasts lead us to the last one. Until now, Daniel has referred to real animals that actually exist and to which we can relate. We've all seen lions, bears, and leopards. But Daniel had nothing to relate the last beast to, for it was so perverse that nothing in the known world was like it.

The first three kingdoms, violent and evil as they were, still took pride in showing some kindness to those they conquered. It was their custom to always take the best, the wealthiest, the wisest men into their fold. Cyrus of the Medo-Persians took pride in helping re-establish the religions of those who had been conquered.

In contrast, Rome was ruthless. It took pride in trampling and destroying everything that represented the conquered people. Thus the Romans made no effort to preserve the integrity – and sometimes even the memory – of those they exterminated. This certainly describes the first phase of the Roman Empire, and will also describe the second phase that will be led by the false messiah sometime in our future. More importantly, keep in mind that this will be a hallmark of the false messiah. He will present himself as a man of peace, but his "peace" will be entirely defined by himself. His "peace" might not look much like *your* peace.

Daniel 7:7 tells us:

> After this I kept looking in the night visions, and behold, a fourth beast, dreadful and terrifying and extremely strong; and it had large iron teeth. It devoured and crushed and trampled down the remainder with its feet; and it was different from all the beasts that were before it, and it had ten horns.

This beast is described as having ten horns. In Hebrew the word for horn has a metaphorical meaning that represents authority or a nation. So this beast will somehow encompass ten kings or ten nations, or ten autonomous regions on the globe, and the authority that comes with each of them. In Revelation 13 we encounter another beast that had ten horns as well. Are these two beasts one and the same? Probably so.

In the book of Daniel as well as in Revelation 13, we see that authority to rule will be given to Daniel's fourth beast for 3-1/2 years. With this authority, this beast that we further encounter in the book of Revelation represents the false messiah and will make war on God's people.

> It was also given to him to make war with the saints and to overcome them, and authority over every tribe and people and tongue and nation was given to him. (Revelation 13:7)

> I kept looking, and that horn was waging war with the saints and overpowering them. (Daniel 7:21)

> He will speak out against the Most High and wear down the saints of the Highest One, and he will intend to make alterations in times and in law; and they will be given into his hand for a time, times, and half a time. (Daniel 7:25)

As in the book of Revelation, when God describes this same beast in Daniel, that beast also has a false prophet (Revelation 19:20). In Daniel 7:8, this false prophet is described as "a horn that comes up amongst the other ten." It says that this horn, or false prophet, will destroy three of the ten horns and will have eyes like a man and a mouth that speaks great things. In Revelation 13 we see, in fact, that this is true He is even able to "speak down" fire from heaven like the prophet Elijah of old. This is a lesson that we should learn in how to determine words, or prophecies, that come from God. Circumstances and/or miraculous power are not among the signs that prove that a prophet or a sign is truly from God.

How to Determine Whether a Dream, a Vision, a Feeling, or an Impression Has Merit

- Does it line up with God's Word? (Deuteronomy 13:1–4)

- Does the messenger have a history of having his messages come true? (Deuteronomy 18:20–22) Does the messenger speak in the name of other gods?

- Is the messenger himself living an exemplary life? Is he attempting to follow the ways of God? (Jeremiah 23:10,14)

- Is the messenger countering the Word of God? For example, is he speaking blessings when no blessing has been earned, when in fact the Bible promised a curse for doing such things or behaving in such a manner? (Jeremiah 23:17)

- A word should come in an orderly manner or environment. (1 Corinthians 14:37–40)

We know that this fourth beast lives in the final days before the second coming of the Messiah. Daniel 7:9–14 describes God's coming at the conclusion of this last evil empire. We see God setting up His kingdom and judging the beast and those who do not have their names written in the Book of Life. The body of the beast is destroyed and given over to be burnt with fire, and his power is taken away by the one Daniel 7:13 refers to as "the Ancient of Days," which is another description for God Himself.

This fourth beast will be destroyed at the hand of God, in contrast to the previous three, who were destroyed by each other.

The Ancient of Days and the Son of Man

In Daniel 7:9 and 13, we see the Messiah being described as the Ancient of Days, which equates Him with God. But He is also being described as the Son of Man, which equates Him with Yeshua. This phrase, the "son of man," during the time of the life of Yeshua (Jesus), was the most common phrase used to refer to the Messiah. It was an Aramaic phrase, pronounced *bar enash*.

It was not the equivalent of any son that a father might have. No Hebrew would refer to themselves or anyone else as a "son of man." This name for the Messiah evolved out of this passage right here in Daniel 7, and became the common name referring to the Messiah during the time of Yeshua.

In the New Testament we commonly see Yeshua being referred to as the "Son of Man." Now we understand why this statement is so profound. From our English perspective, this phrase is not particularly meaningful and certainly doesn't stand out in our minds as a designation for God because all males are sons of men. But from a Hebrew mindset, this is a radical pronouncement. That is why the Jews of Yeshua's day were constantly accusing Him of blasphemy and sometimes picking up stones to punish Him for the same.

Daniel 7:25 tells us:

> He will speak out against the Most High and wear down the saints of the Highest One, and he will intend to make alterations in times and in law; and they will be given into his hand for a time, times, and half a time.

This passage is very intriguing. It conveys certain things that this person (antichrist/false messiah) will do. It says that he will wear out the saints of God and attempt to change the times and the law. Recall that Daniel chapters 2–7 were originally written in Aramaic. The Aramaic word here for time is *zeman*, which means "a set time."[2] Its root means "appointed time."[3] Recall, also, that in Genesis 1:14 it says:

> Then God said, "Let there be lights in the expanse of the heavens to separate the day from the night, and let them be for signs and for seasons and for days and years."

Here, the word for "seasons" is *mo'ed*. This word is acting as the equivalent for the Aramaic word that Daniel used, for it as well means "a set time" or "appointed time." This Hebrew word, and we believe the Aramaic word as well, is used by God to designate the seven festivals that he asked His people to celebrate throughout each calendar year. These are "appointed times" because God intended to have special meetings with you and me on these days. He has determined that they are special to Him. We should therefore show up to honor what is special to God.

Many in the church of today believe that these appointed times, or festivals that God has put in his day timer to meet with us, have been abolished. The first question I have is, "Why would the church want to abolish the very concept of having special meetings with God?"

But more importantly, if they have already been abolished, why is God at the end of time making a big deal out of the fact that the *beast* is abolishing them? If He had already abolished them Himself, why would it be such a big deal (or *even possible*) for the beast to abolish them all over again?

But it gets worse. The text above (Daniel 7:25) also tells us that this beast will attempt to change the law as well. The underlying Aramaic word here for "law" is *dat*[4]. The word *dat* occurs in both the Aramaic as well as in the Hebrew language, and in both cases it means the same thing, essentially referring to the laws and edicts of God. So, God is obviously referring to the law described in Torah. Again we ask the same question that we asked just above. If the false messiah is so evil by abolishing the law, as well as God's feasts (or appointed times), what makes it okay when the church does the same thing? And if the laws have been abolished at the death and resurrection of Yeshua, why do they need to be re-abolished by the false messiah?

The pictography piles on additional conviction to those in the "abolish the laws of God" camp. Law is spelled *dalet-tav*. Recall that this represents the laws of God. The pictography says that the laws of God are the pathway to the sign of the covenant. The ancient tav took the form of a cross, and so the sign of the covenant was fulfilled by Yeshua when He came as the sacrificial lamb and allowed himself to be hung on the tav, or that old rugged cross.

So how does God want us to approach Him? Certainly with humility and recognition that we have sinned. But He also wants us to make a commitment that we are going to start shaking up our lives in conformity with His principles for holy living, which are defined as *His law*.

No, our efforts don't bring salvation. Only faith in Yeshua does that. But they do bring a state of holiness and earn us the white garments that God gives to His bride in Revelation 19:8:

> It was given to her to clothe herself in fine linen, bright and clean; for the fine linen is the righteous acts of the saints.

Here we see clearly that it is the bride's acts, or her works — but not her faith — that earn her the bridal garment. What do you suppose those who do no righteous acts will earn? What do you suppose those who have all their works burned up will earn?

The passage below makes it clear that they are still believers and go to be with Him, but there is no other reward.

> [10]According to the grace of God which was given to me, like a wise master builder I laid a foundation and another is building on it. But each man must be careful how he builds on it. [11] For no man can lay a foundation other than the one which is laid, which is Jesus Christ. [12] Now if any man builds

on the foundation with gold, silver, precious stones, wood, hay, straw, [13] each man's work will become evident; for the day will show it because it is to be revealed with fire, and the fire itself will test the quality of each man's work. [14] If any man's work which he has built on it remains, he will receive a reward. [15] If any man's work is burned up, he will suffer loss; but he himself will be saved, yet so as through fire. (1 Corinthians 3:10–15)

To repeat our main point one more time. If Satan, via the false messiah, is in opposition to God's laws and His feasts and will attempt to cancel them himself, in what spirit is the work of the church being done when it tries to accomplish the same?

6
The Two-Horned Goat
(Daniel 8)

There was one memory that Daniel just loved to replay. Whenever he had the chance he also liked to bring it up when he was around his friends, Shadrack, Meshach, and Abednego. On the other hand, they didn't really want to hear it again, especially Daniel's rendition. But Daniel would tell the story anyway, adding a few embellishments that everyone would laugh at and sometimes argue about. But in the end it was all in good fun.

In actuality, the days from which that memory came were fateful times – not much fun at all. There were always people who seemed to think more highly about themselves than is wise. You know the type – the guy who is full of himself yet gives not a hoot about other people's feelings or opinions. Why? Because he thinks he already knows what is right, such that everyone else's opinion is just more static.

Some people even go too far with all of this and begin believing that they might have descended from some godly line. That is exactly what happened to King Nebuchadnezzar. After hearing the interpretation of his dream involving the statue made of four types of metal, things may have started to go awry in the king's mind, especially after learning that he himself was the head of gold on that statue! Thus he started to toy with delusions of grandeur. Unfortunately, once you dwell on something long enough, especially when you believe that your vision came from God, your vision of reality can go south.

Perhaps that is why King Nebuchadnezzar ordered that an image of gold should be made, standing almost 100 feet tall when it was finished! That it was made completely of gold didn't fool anyone as to whom the statue represented. Worse than that, everyone in his kingdom was ordered to bow down and worship it upon pain of death. Daniel just happened to be visiting another province that day or he would have been swept up in the "fun" too.

Most of the king's underlings just went along and obeyed. Why lose your life when all the king wanted was for you to bend your knee and recognize his greatness, right? Well, there are always a few stand-outs. Just like God never allowed Daniel to blend in, so too with Shadrack, Meshach, and Abednego. They would not bow to a manmade idol even to save their lives.

The pain-of-death penalty for not worshiping the statue was an immediate trip into the furnace of blazing fire. And that is exactly what happened to Daniel's friends. The only problem was that they wouldn't ignite. And when the king saw them in the blazing furnace there appeared to be a fourth person in there as well! This, of course, astonished the king and everyone else who saw what was happening.

At this point the king began to get a clue that maybe someone else was bigger than he was. The king certainly knew that he didn't have power over the flames. He felt the fire singeing his face as he got as close as he could to the furnace, to confirm that there were indeed four people in there. After calling for all of them to come out, and then observing their state, he began to understand the truth. They were just fine. Their cloths were just fine. Even their hair was fine — nothing was singed even a little bit. In fact, they didn't even smell of smoke.

Through this event God became known to the king once again. Sometimes we all take a bit of time to realize that there truly is, in fact, a God. And He very much wants us to give our attention to Him. In fact, what God wants is actually something more than just attention. He wants us to love, adore, and pursue Him with all of our hearts, minds, and strength. Yes, God wants us to have a relationship with Him. But in order to do that we need to realize that He is God, not we ourselves. We are not the ultimate determining factor in our lives. He is.

To some extent the king did that. He was certainly awed and followed that with a decree that everyone in the world should not speak anything amiss against the God of Shadrach, Meshach, and Abednego. Yet at the same time King Nebuchadnezzar proclaimed that if anyone did speak amiss they would be cut to pieces and their houses would be made into dunghills. This was exactly how God does NOT want people coming to Him. He has given us all a choice which He will never take away, and He certainly does not want us to come to Him through fear and threats.

Unfortunately, this is how the kingdom of darkness works. Through temptation, intimidation, and threats, Satan distracts mankind from the truth and causes us to deviate from what should be our true course. And that true course leads straight to God Himself.

Meanwhile love, kindness, patience, and truth draw us closer in relationship to the Creator Himself.

Recall that there are seven dreams, or visions, in the book of Daniel. If we overlay these seven dreams and correlate them with the seven lights on the menorah, the prophecy in chapter 8 is the fourth one and would be the equivalent of the central light of the menorah. This center light is called the *shamash*, the same word the Hebrews used to describe the sun overhead. It also is a word used to describe the Messiah, because He is the Light of the World.

This is important to realize because, in this chapter, we have the first prophecy that gives us lots of information about the *false* messiah. The false messiah will soon claim to be the Light of the World. So, in these seven prophecies that God has given mankind through Daniel, He reveals the plan of Satan. And part of the plan of Satan is to masquerade as God Himself. Satan's claim to be God is a copycat of the shamash position of the fourth dream.

The prophecy in Daniel 8 describes the second and third kingdoms of the four kingdoms represented in the previous chapter. A ram is used to denote the second, the Medo-Persian Empire, whereas a he-goat is used to describe the third, Alexander the Great's Greek Empire. This ram is seen expanding its empire westward, northward, and southward. This is exactly what the Medo-Persian Empire did. It expanded north and west into Greece, and southward all the way down to Egypt. But it was confronted by the he-goat, or Alexander the Great, which broke the ram's horn and made it powerless to defend itself against the Greek Empire, again aligning perfectly with history.

Within ten years Alexander the Great had conquered the entire land mass that the Medo-Persians had taken decades to conquer. This prophecy also describes in greater detail what happened to Alexander the Great and his empire after his life was cut off at an early age. It also explains more about the four horns that rose up after Alexander died and became nations unto themselves.

The Exploits of Antiochus

One of those nations was the Seleucid Empire, which came out of the split-up of Alexander's empire into four pieces. The Seleucid Empire is described here as a horn that rises up and becomes "exceedingly great," growing to the south and the east. This is exactly how Antiochus Epiphanes expanded his empire which today would be the lands in and around Syria. He moved south, conquering Israel first, then Egypt, and also extended his empire into Iran to the east.

> [10]It grew up to the host of heaven and caused some of the host and some of the stars to fall to the earth, and it trampled them down. [11] It even magnified itself to be equal with the Commander of the host; and it removed the regular sacrifice from Him, and the place of His sanctuary was thrown down. [12] And on account of transgression the host will be given over to the horn along with the regular sacrifice; and it will fling truth to the ground and perform its will and prosper (Daniel 8:10–12)

These verses describe the exploits of Antiochus, but they also deal with the false messiah and describe what he will do in the end times. Revelation 13 and 17 give us parallel information with these passages in Daniel. They both talk about a beast who looks like a man but is actually indwelt by Satan who shall rise up and conquer the world and will attempt to magnify himself by claiming to be the true God in heaven.

7
The Seventy-Week Prophecy
(Daniel 9)

S ometimes people think that they're something special when they
are just people like the rest of us. No, they're not the sun, giving us
light so we can find our way. We can do that just fine, thank you very
much. Yes, they sometimes have more money and influence, but when
they don't realize that these powers come with greater responsibility,
that's when things go awry.

Daniel recalled that it was not just King Belshazzar or King Nebuchadnezzar who had problems with wealth and power. The last king of Judah
had fallen for this age-old temptation, too.

The king didn't live up to his name. Zedekiah means "my righteousness
is Yahweh," but Zedekiah wasn't righteous at all. He was exactly the opposite: he was truly an evil man. King Nebuchadnezzar appointed him
as king of Judah, but all Zedekiah did was cause trouble for the ruling
powers in Babylon. It came to a head when he rebelled against them.

Zedekiah didn't want to submit to the punishment dealt out by God.
If we are patient during times of trouble, even trouble God allows into
our lives to bring correction, good usually comes. But that was not
what the king chose. He thought that he could bring about freedom for
himself and his country by going his own way, but by rebelling against

King Nebuchadnezzar he was actually rebelling against God. And this caused even more trouble to rain down on him and Judea.

The armies of Babylon returned again, but this time they were not nearly as "benevolent" as they had been before, having left the country and Jerusalem, its capital, standing. The people were exiled, the city was razed, and worst of all, the precious house of YHWH, the temple, was destroyed.

All this happened because one man did not turn his heart and mind to God. Or, maybe it was something more. Maybe the people of Judea were at fault, too. They had been warned by God. He had even sent them a holy king, Josiah, who had ruled for 31 years prior to King Zedekiah's reign. God loved how King Josiah had tried to turn the people back to Himself by functioning as an example in the way he governed.

But the people would not listen and would not turn their hearts to God. So, God eventually brought the judgment that He had so long ago warned them about. That warning was first found in the ancient book of Deuteronomy, and it was fulfilled in Daniel's day.

What Daniel had learned through all the visions, dreams, and interpretations he had received is that people will be people. It seems that all men, in whatever age they live, tend to want to believe the same lie – they can live their lives any way they want because there is no one to be accountable to in the end. Certainly those to come in the final age would believe this way too.

God had told Daniel that in this last age knowledge would increase, but it wouldn't help. God would reveal Himself even more clearly, with an increase of His power manifested in their midst. God would bring an increase in evidence for His existence and the truth found in Torah, but most people would fall away. What was it that the power of darkness had over mankind, anyway?

Throughout the ages of men there have always arisen leaders who wave their fists against the Creator. A common trait that these leaders share is the false notion that they themselves are gods or are born from gods.

According to Daniel's vision, the very last ruler of the ages will share this trait. In fact, he will actually claim to be the God of Daniel and will seat himself in YHWH's temple.

Daniel knew that this last king would unite the entire world against God. He would entice the people by playing to their passions. And, in spite of the increase in knowledge in the days to come, there will not be a corresponding increase in wisdom. The last generation will be so dumbed down that they won't be able to tell right from wrong. Actually, many will believe that there really is no right or wrong, except what each supposes for himself. The evidence for the truth will be everywhere, but very few will see it. This evil ruler will promote ideas that are exactly opposite to the laws of nature and the admonishments of God, leading people to behave like beasts.

Maybe that was it. Maybe this last despot would be something other than a "normal" man. Daniel had come in contact with personified evil and knew that it was very real. The Torah revealed that God called that evil "the serpent, Satan." He was once an angel but had fallen from God's presence because of his pride and the sin he pursued.

Daniel had seen firsthand the result of similar delusions in men's minds when they were overwhelmed by pride. He now wondered if this fallen cherub might also believe, because of his pride, that he could alter the plans of God by defeating Him. Was Satan thinking that he, in fact, was God, himself? Was he really powerful enough to challenge God?

Daniel knew that his God was all-powerful. Otherwise, why had the serpent lost and been eternally cursed by God at the confrontation in the Garden of Eden? Why did God seem to always have the upper hand whenever He confronted the powers of darkness in Torah? Pharaoh certainly was acting on the serpent's behalf and using its power, yet he lost miserably. No, YHWH was the Creator and He was all powerful . . . period.

Daniel 9 contains Daniel's fifth vision. It came to Daniel in the first year of the reign of Darius. Darius was the governor put in place by

Cyrus after taking Babylon from King Belshazzar, Nebuchadnezzar's grandson. Darius's reign began in 539 BC.

> [8] "The prophets who were before me and before you from ancient times prophesied against many lands and against great kingdoms, of war and of calamity and of pestilence. [9] The prophet who prophesies of peace, when the word of the prophet comes to pass, then that prophet will be known as one whom the LORD has truly sent."
>
> [10] Then Hananiah the prophet took the yoke from the neck of Jeremiah the prophet and broke it. [11] Hananiah spoke in the presence of all the people, saying, "Thus says the LORD, 'Even so will I break within two full years the yoke of Nebuchadnezzar king of Babylon from the neck of all the nations.'" Then the prophet Jeremiah went his way.
>
> [12] The word of the LORD came to Jeremiah after Hananiah the prophet had broken the yoke from off the neck of the prophet Jeremiah. (Jeremiah 28:8–12)

The above passage is a prophecy that was given to Jeremiah many decades before Daniel's time and was now coming to fruition. It foretold the disobedience of God's people to His ways and that they would be exiled to Babylon for 70 years. The prophecy goes on to explain that the Israelites would be set free again after those 70 years and would be allowed to go back to their homeland.

The length of this 70-year exile was due to Israel's failure to honor the sabbatical year which occurs every seven years. God had long before instructed Israel to leave the land fallow and rest from their labors on the sabbatical year, just as they were to rest on the Sabbath. He promised that if they obeyed His commandment He would multiply their harvest at the end of the sixth year, thereby providing for their needs until the next harvest, two years later.

Because the sabbatical year wasn't kept for 70 sabbatical years of the preceding 490-year period, God now enforced the consequences of violating His laws. His people replaced a blessing for a curse due to their disobedience. God's law will be enforced in the end, either willingly on our part or through bondage.

It Wasn't the First Time!

This was not the first time that God used a 490-year period. He models this length of time again and again and again in the biblical past. A scholar by the name of Clarence Larkin first came up with this observation.[1] Although I question some of his dates and certainly disagree with his dispensational views, the idea that God works with His people in 490 year segments is novel. From Abraham to the Exodus was 490 years. From the Exodus to the first temple was 490 years. From the temple to the first edict by Artaxerxes to rebuild Jerusalem was 490 years. And then from Artaxerxes's edict to the first coming of Yeshua the Messiah was 490 years.

This is modeled even in Yeshua's statement about how many times people should forgive each other. He told them they should forgive seven times seventy, which is 490 times (Matthew 18:22). Is God hinting, again, that we should be like Him? We see that His patience many times lasts for about 490 years. He gives us that much time to try to get it right. And if we don't, judgment seems to fall.

Daniel 9 describes the 490-year period as a seventy-week decree that is placed on the people and the Holy City. As we will see, this seventy-year period is broken down into weeks, with each week equaling seven years. So this seventy-week prophecy encompasses another 490-year period.

Daniel 9:25 tells us when this 490-year period will start. It says that there will be a decree to restore and rebuild Jerusalem which will initiate the beginning of this 490-year period. The previous verse, verse 24, describes how this 490-year period will end. The text says:

> Seventy weeks have been decreed for your people and your holy city, to finish the transgression, to make an end of sin, to make atonement for iniquity, to bring in everlasting

righteousness, to seal up vision and prophecy and to anoint the most holy place. (Daniel 9:24)

God is describing His final work in Daniel 9:24, which will usher in His kingdom and initiate His thousand-year reign.

Obviously God's final work has not yet occurred, but the decree to restore and rebuild Jerusalem has. In fact, it has happened twice. It occurred first in 445 BC. On March 14 of that year, Artaxerxes, the king of the Medes and the Persians, made a decree that gave permission for the Jews to restore Jerusalem and its walls. This decree should not be confused with the law that Cyrus passed, allowing the Jews to go back to Jerusalem and rebuild the temple in approximately 536 BC.

Embedded within the seventy-week prophecy was a sixty-nine week period composed of a time of 7 weeks and a time of 62 weeks, for a total of 69 weeks:

> [25] So you are to know and discern that from the issuing of a decree to restore and rebuild Jerusalem until Messiah the Prince there will be seven weeks and sixty-two weeks; it will be built again, with plaza and moat, even in times of distress. (Daniel 9:25)

These weeks were not composed of seven days but of seven years. The Hebrew word for week can mean a period of seven days or seven years.[2] Multiplying seven times 69 gives 483 years for the Daniel 9:25 prophecy of the coming of the Messiah to be fulfilled.

Some people then take 445 BC, add 483 years to it, and arrive at AD 38. However, nothing of any particular interest occurred in AD 38, especially in regard to this prophecy. From verse 24 we can determine that the end of this 483-year period will bring an atonement for iniquity. As we know, iniquity was atoned for at the death and resurrection of Yeshua, which was in AD 32.

When describing time, God does not use our Gregorian calendar. Nor does He use our calendar years. He uses the ancient Hebrew calendar, with days and years determined by it. So, in order to properly understand and apply the Daniel 9:25 prophecy about 483 years, we need to convert those years, as defined in the Hebrew calendar, into modern Gregorian dates. In doing so we need to convert 483 Hebrew years into days, in which case we arrive at 173,880 days. If we then add those days to March 14, 445 BC, which was when the proclamation to go and rebuild Jerusalem and its walls was issued, we arrive at Passover Lamb Selection Day. This is better known in the Christian world as the day of the Triumphal Entry into Jerusalem, Palm Sunday.

Lamb Selection Day always occurred on Nisan 10, a Sunday in AD 32, five days, including Sunday, before the Passover and Yeshua's crucifixion in AD 32. From the very first Passover, the Israelites would go out to the flocks and select a pure, unblemished one-year-old lamb five days before the Passover. They would then bring that lamb into their home where it would live with the family like a pet.

Unfortunately, five days later, the lambs were sacrificed and the whole family was required to eat their pet. We bring this up only to highlight the point that God was making by requiring His people to do this. Metaphorically speaking, He was the Lamb. He wants us to realize what the price for sin really is: it was necessary for our best friend to die on the cross to pay the price for our sins.

Are We Just Like the Pharisees?

> [1]The Pharisees and Sadducees came up, and testing Jesus, they asked Him to show them a sign from heaven. [2]But He replied to them, "When it is evening, you say, 'It will be fair weather, for the sky is red.' [3]And in the morning, 'There will be a storm today, for the sky is red and threatening.' Do you know how to discern the appearance of the sky, but cannot discern the signs of the times?" (Matthew 16:1–3)

Just before Yeshua was crucified He came to Jerusalem and entered into various discussions with the Pharisees and the Sadducees. In the passage above He is confronted with requests to perform a miracle or a sign in the heavens. His answer is very interesting, especially in

Hebrew. He calls his questioners hypocrites because they can discern the signs for the weather but they can't see the signs of the times.

The words in this passage for "sign" and "time" are *ot* and *mo'ed*. In Hebrew the word *ot* means "a portent, a telling of something that is going to come in the future."[3] The word *mo'ed* means an "appointed time" or "a set time."[4] What He is really saying to the Pharisees here, is that you can see the signs for the weather, but you, the ones who've been given the responsibility of understanding Torah and teaching it to the people, are missing the appointed time that I instructed you about through prophecy.

What prophecy is Yeshua referring to here? I believe He's specifically referring to the seventy-week prophecy in Daniel 9:25. This prophecy says that from the going forth of the proclamation to restore and rebuild Jerusalem there shall be 69 weeks, or 483 years.

To properly understand biblical passages of time, as explained above, we must convert everything to the Hebrew calendar. This will allow us to determine, just as the Pharisees and Sadducees should have determined, the exact time of the Triumphal Entry to the very day. The Passover Lamb Selection Day, the day of His public arrival to Jerusalem, and the day that this prophecy in Daniel predicted, was a very unique and important day to the Hebrews. On this day they would lead all the lambs that had met the purity requirements up the hill to Jerusalem to prepare for slaughter.

> . . . [7] and brought the donkey and the colt, and laid their coats on them; and He sat on the coats. [8] Most of the crowd spread their coats in the road, and others were cutting branches from the trees and spreading them in the road. [9]The crowds going ahead of Him, and those who followed, were shouting,
>
> "Hosanna to the Son of David;
> BLESSED IS HE WHO COMES IN THE NAME OF THE LORD;
> Hosanna in the highest!"

[10] When He had entered Jerusalem, all the city was stirred, saying, "Who is this?" (Matthew 21:7–10)

In the process the people would line the road and lay down palm branches for the lambs to walk on. This is important because in ancient times, people from all over the Mideast, in efforts to honor their king when he entered their city, would do the same thing. Why would Israelites lay down palm branches for lambs to walk on? Because they realized that these lambs represented the prophesied Messiah who was going to come and free them from their bondage. These lambs were joined by our Messiah, Yeshua, on that fateful Triumphal Entry Day. The crowds yelled out to Him, "Hosanna! Hosanna!"

Hosanna is adapted from Hebrew and means "Save us, we pray!" The "raw" meaning is "salvation." In reality, they were actually saying "Hoshea," which has as its root the word "Yasha," which means "to be delivered or saved."[5] This word is the root word for "Yeshua," Jesus' real Hebrew name. So, as Yeshua our Messiah, who was named "salvation," was riding on the way to the temple to be sacrificed a few days later, the people were yelling out "Salvation!" to the only man who could, in fact, save them. That was their messiah – and ours – who had been given the name Yeshua, which meant salvation.

The Name of Our Lord, God, and Messiah

The name "Yeshua" is more profound than the translated name "Jesus."[6] "Jesus" has no underlying meaning in either Hebrew or Greek or English. It's a construct of sounds that evolved from Hebrew, to Greek, to Latin, and then to English. For example, there is no letter in the Hebrew alphabet that makes the "j" sound. The value in knowing God's real name in Hebrew is to recognize the linkage that His name has with other important passages we find in the Bible that make mention of that name.

Without knowing the linkage you'll never see when certain passages are making reference to the Messiah. The name "Jesus" just can't help you in that capacity. On another level, "Yeshua" is spelled *yud-shin-vav-ayin* in Hebrew letters. As we've learned, all of these letters are pictographs, and when you string together the meaning of the pictographs in Yeshua's name it communicates something unique about what our Savior has done for us. The pictographs for the letters in Yeshua's name tell us His name means "the work that consumes the covenant of your eyes (or what you see)."

This also links back to the fall of man. Genesis 3:5–6 tells us:

> [5] "For God knows that in the day you eat from it your eyes will be opened, and you will be like God, knowing good and evil." [6] When the woman saw that the tree was good for food, and that it was a delight to the eyes, and that the tree was desirable to make one wise, she took from its fruit and ate; and she gave also to her husband with her, and he ate.

The snake communicated to Eve that upon eating the forbidden fruit and violating God's instructions, her eyes would be opened – "and you will be like God, knowing good and evil." And she saw, with her eyes, that the fruit was pleasant. Adam and Eve, as well as all the rest of mankind throughout the ages, have continued to make covenants with their eyes, determining for themselves what is good. In so doing we have made a covenant with sin and death. Embedded in our Messiah's name is the work that frees us from the bondage of our sin, for His name communicates that HE will perform the work that will consume that very bondage — that attachment — that we have to the covenant of sin and death.

Yeshua chided the Pharisees and Sadducees in Matthew 16:3 because they would have known that March 14, 445 BC was the date where a proclamation was made to rebuild Jerusalem that established the beginning of the seventy-week prophecy. Artaxerxes I, the king over the Medes and the Persians, conquered almost the entire Middle East and the lands beyond. By a stroke of the pen, on this very day —March 14, 445 BC —he signed a law giving permission for the Israelites to return to Jerusalem, restore its walls, and resettle the city. From that day on, by counting the days contained in 483 Hebrew years, any Bible student – and especially the religious leaders – would arrive at the very day Yeshua was being hailed as King and called upon to save the people. It shouldn't have been a surprise.

Seven Weeks and 62 Weeks

Daniel 9:25 tells us that the 69-weeks is cut up into two time periods — a seven-week period, equaling 49 years, and a 62-week period, equaling 434 years. The 69 weeks represent 483 years. Why is this 483-year period cut up into a 49-year time period and a 434-year time period?

Historians have not been able to identify anything unique that occurred at the end of the 49-year period, which would have started in 445 BC and ended in the year 396 BC. There's no time gap between the 49 and 434 years because they are continuous. They foretell the exact day of His Triumphal Entry.

The prevailing opinion among Christians is that chapter 9 of Daniel should be understood in the following manner. There are two time periods, a 69-week period (483 years) and a one-week period (seven years), equaling 70 weeks (490 years).

However, there is another interpretation that has developed which gives a completely different perspective, adding a whole new dimension to the analysis of the Second Coming. I believe that the one-week and 62-week time periods are each preceded by a seven-week (49-year) period. Daniel 9:25 tells us that the seven-week period begins with a proclamation allowing God's people to go back to Jerusalem. If there are two 49-year periods, then there should have been two proclamations to go and restore Jerusalem recorded in history. There was such a proclamation in 445 BC. Have there been any others?

Indeed there was. The Israeli Six-Day War was a monumental victory for Israel because they gained Jerusalem and other key territories. The last day of that war was June 11, 1967, followed by the Knesset's (i.e., the Israeli parliament, or congress) proclamation stating that the

Israelis now had the right to return and restore Jerusalem. Adding the number of days in 49 Hebrew years to June 11, 1967 arrives at September 23, 2015, the festival of Yom Kippur, the Day of Judgment. Among Jews and others who still celebrate this festival, it is widely known that on this day the Book of Life is closed. No more time is given for repentance and getting things right with God. Your name is either in the Book of Life . . . or it isn't.

We are not trying to say that beyond September 23, 2015, God will no longer receive new converts into His kingdom. But what we are trying to emphasize is that on some future day, maybe in the near future, there will come a day in which there will be no more time for repentance. The invitation to be part of His kingdom will have been turned down for the last time.

The interesting thing about this understanding of the text is how it aligns the Second Coming with the fall festival days, something we fully expect to occur because of the significance of His festivals and how He has fulfilled them in the past. Adding one week (or seven Hebrew years' worth of days) to September 23, 2015, would point to the fall of 2022 for the arrival, the Second Coming, of the Messiah. Granted, this is just one interpretation among several that could be made.

However, as God gave detailed information to the ancient Pharisees so they wouldn't miss His return, so also has God given people today specific information so they don't miss the Second Coming.

The Last Week

This last seven-year sabbatical period, beginning in 2015 on Yom Kippur, and ending in the fall of 2022, is described by the verse that follows:

> [27] "And he will make a firm covenant with the many for one week, but in the middle of the week he will put a stop to sacrifice and grain offering; and on the wing of abominations will come one who makes desolate, even until a complete

destruction, one that is decreed, is poured out on the one who makes desolate." (Daniel 9:27)

Paul, in II Thessalonians 2:1–4, refers to these concluding events:

> [1] Now we request you, brethren, with regard to the coming of our Lord Jesus Christ and our gathering together to Him, [2] that you not be quickly shaken from your composure or be disturbed either by a spirit or a message or a letter as if from us, to the effect that the day of the Lord has come. [3] Let no one in any way deceive you, for it will not come unless the apostasy comes first, and the man of lawlessness is revealed, the son of destruction, [4] who opposes and exalts himself above every so-called god or object of worship, so that he takes his seat in the temple of God, displaying himself as being God.

Here we see the beast being called "the man of lawlessness," or "Torah-lessness." He is described as one who will oppose and exalt himself above all gods and will take God's seat in the temple, displaying himself as "the real God." God allows this charade, the worst deception of all time, to continue for 3-1/2 years.

Following the Law Is Just Old Testament Stuff . . . Or Is It?

The Greek word for lawless in II Thessalonias 2:3 is *anomos*. Greek words preceded by an "a" add the idea of "no," or "law<u>less</u>." *Nomos* is the word the ancient translators of the Septuagint used to translate the word "Torah" into Greek. Paul is saying that the beast (the antichrist) will be someone who completely disregards Torah, or the English word that is used to translate Torah, "law."

The church of today believes that when Jesus came, He abolished "the law." But in our passage, Paul is denigrating the antichrist for doing exactly the same. How will the claims of a future false

---

messiah that the law has been abolished act as a sign? The church may just say, "We already knew that!"

We believe that there is a huge contrast between these two messiahs. One came and promoted the law. The other will come and is described as the lawless one, for the very purpose of our being able to single him out. Without knowing the laws of God, people will not be able to differentiate and contrast the two. That's why this is a sign.

Paul delineates two events that will occur just before the Second Coming – one is of a general nature, and one is specific. The first event is the general one, described as a great falling away in II Thessalonians 2:3. Many believers will fall away en masse from the truth and from their salvation during the days that lead up to the Second Coming. The specific event is when the beast takes up residence on God's throne in the temple and claims to be the very God of the Bible. Then Messiah will come.

As the Scripture above tells us, this beast's act of taking up God's identity will be one of the last signs before the Second Coming. This sign would require us to be here in order for us to observe it. Consequently, the last half of the last seven years will make known to mankind the two witnesses as well as the beast that will usher in the abomination of God's temple.

As you can see, the implication here is that many terrible troubles will come upon the earth while believers in the true God are still here. Are you ready?

8

Angelic Warfare
(Daniel 10)

Daniel had learned firsthand what spiritual influences and battles were all about. Several times he had received a message directly from God. The problem was that he truly didn't understand all that was being conveyed. That's why an angel came to him and helped him comprehend. Later, he began to suspect that his "helper" was a bit more than an angel. In truth He was actually the Messiah.

Among other things, this "Angel" told Daniel that He had been detained for twenty-one days by a being called the Prince of the kingdom of Persia who was a fallen angel serving the power of darkness. What was even more curious was that Daniel had been fasting during that same twenty-one day period.

Daniel remembered that when he first arrived in Babylon his masters had tried to give him food from the king's table. This would have sounded good to most people, but not to someone who ate a diet prescribed by God. His masters had laughed when he asked to substitute his own diet for the king's food, calling it the equivalent of a fast. Yet Daniel knew full well that limiting his diet to what God called food was not a fast. It was just eating food as God defined it. All else was not fit for man.

Also, whenever Daniel prayed — especially about really important issues that were on his heart — sometimes he would fast as well. He knew that his God had admonished His people to pray and fast in pursuit of greater closeness with Him. Daniel discovered that he felt better afterward. The practice of fasting regularly had an amazing impact on his overall health and energy.

Even more important, submitting himself in this way to God brought a closer relationship with the Father. There was another spiritual benefit, too. Daniel found it easier to fend off temptations that the minions of darkness did their best to "shoot into his mind." Fasting seemed to diminish the power of the bondages that would have come from giving in to his own or the enemy's ways.

His prayers would be answered even though God did not always say yes. Yet whatever He said was sure to bring clarity and direction. Sometimes God would even congratulate him for a job well done.

The last three chapters of Daniel — 10, 11, and 12 — explain the final two visions of the seven that are contained in the book of Daniel. These two visions are actually one vision split up into two parts. The first part is in chapter 11 and includes history that occurred between 300 BC and 150 BC. The second part, mostly explained in chapter 12, gives information about the very end of time before the second coming of Messiah.

Quite possibly, the reason for this two-part presentation was that these two visions (which, again, are actually one) are describing, first, an archetype of the antichrist. That part is being played by what is now, to us, a historical figure, Antiochus Epiphanes. The second part then describes the *actual* false messiah.

By studying what are now historical facts about Antiochus Epiphanes we can learn many things about what the false messiah's exploits will actually be — how he will govern, how he will manage his kingdom, and how he will confront those who oppose him.

Chapter 10 acts as an introductory chapter, giving us some very insight-ful information about the spirit world. In his two-part vision, Daniel is visited by spirit beings who make presentations giving great insight into future events. And, they explain to him the battles that they have struggled through to present this information to him.

This vision occurs in the third year of King Cyrus of Persia, who had just conquered Babylon, the city that Daniel lived in up to that point. These details allow us to establish the date that this vision was received as 536 BC. Daniel was given a message of a great future conflict, but he had no idea what it meant. Verse 2 tells us that after hearing the message, Daniel languished, mourned, and lamented for three weeks, foregoing all creature comforts, like food and the ointment customar-ily used after bathing.

The text implies that Daniel was fasting during this 21-day period. When we want to petition God, the Bible instructs us to fast. Grieving, mourning, lamenting, and self-denial can be part of a fast, an all-out effort to get God's attention.

Daniel's Distress

Evidently, Daniel was very distraught at the message he'd been given and wanted additional insight. By directing his thoughts and atten-tion to God during those three weeks, he was trying to get God's ear. God didn't keep Daniel waiting. We know the incredible description of verses 5 and 6 are Yeshua because the New Testament gives these same details (see Revelation 1:12–16, 2:18). In other words, this be-ing who arrived to explain the message to Daniel was actually Yeshua the Messiah.

In the second part of Daniel's vision, which was really a continuation of the first part, this Messenger who came and offered His explanation is referred to as "Adonai." In Daniel's effort to more clearly understand this message, he calls this man "Lord," which is a very typical title used for "The Lord," or God Himself.

> As for me, I heard but could not understand; so I said, "My lord, what will be the outcome of these events?" (Daniel 12:8)

All of this is occurring to Daniel on the shores of the great river Hiddekel, better known today as the Tigris River, which flows south from the mountains of Turkey, through Iraq, and into the Persian Gulf.

So . . . what is going on in part one of this vision? An angel, whom we now know is not an angel but Yeshua Himself, relates that He has been struggling for 21 days to answer Daniel's mournful cry to understand more fully the message he received from God. In Daniel 10:11 God calls out, "Oh Daniel, a man greatly beloved."

Isn't that exactly what *we* want to hear? More importantly, what made Daniel's life stand out? How did he have this kind of rapport with his Maker? Certainly, Daniel was specifically chosen to receive these visions and interpretations and to write the book that bears his name – and not just because he was standing in the right place at the right time. God trusted Daniel and knew he could depend on him. Again and again Daniel had been tried and tested – and he had not been found wanting, such as Belshazzar, the ex-king of Babylon, had been.

But more than that, it's obvious that Daniel had a special relationship with God. It wasn't a knowledge-based relationship alone, but more of a one-on-one relationship that propelled Daniel into this highly esteemed position with God.

What Daniel was about to learn did not affect his own life, nor the lives of the people he knew. The information contained in the visions he was given would impact all of humanity far into the future. And most of it was given by God to Daniel for our own day.

In verse 13 and again in verse 20, Yeshua explains to Daniel that what prevented Him from coming to give Daniel greater insight was the prince of the kingdom of Persia. For 21 days this Prince of Persia was able to prevent God from delivering the message to Daniel. It seems that Michael, the archangel of God whose name means "Who is like

God?", intervened and was able to successfully counteract the forces that opposed the Messiah for those 21 days.

What "Prince" Would Have Such Authority?

So, who is this Prince of Persia who had sufficient authority to oppose God and succeeded in detaining Him? The word for prince, in verses 13 and 20, is *sar*, which means prince and can be used for an archangel.[1] The English word "archangel" is also another word roughly equivalent to the Hebrew word for *cherub*.

As you also may be aware from reading our first book (*Lost in Translation: Rediscovering the Hebrew Roots of Our Faith*), there are three orders of angels: cherubim, seraphim, and teraphim, with the cherubim being the most powerful. They surround God's throne and serve Him constantly.

So, it appears that a fallen angel, who was once a cherub in good standing with God, was now serving Satan's kingdom and therefore tried to oppose God in the deliverance of His message to Daniel. What does this say about the importance of the message? Nowhere else when God gives messages to His prophets in the Bible is there such a monumental struggle, so the message contained in the next two chapters of the book of Daniel just might be important.

Archangels are given jobs by God for His most important purposes. In Genesis 3:24, after Adam and Eve had fallen from grace, God barred the entrance to the Garden of Eden by soliciting one of His mighty cherubim to stand guard with a flaming sword.

One has to wonder why God would need a cherub to guard the Garden of Eden. Couldn't just a regular old angel keep Adam and Eve, mere mortals, from trying to get back in?

Maybe God's purpose wasn't so much to prevent Adam and Eve from re-entering, but to keep out the cherub who caused mankind's whole downfall in the first place: Satan. Of course, Satan wouldn't need to eat the fruit himself. He already is an immortal being. But what a power play he could make by offering this life-restoring fruit to mankind! These people would be drawn to Satan like drug addicts to their supplier. Worst, these folks would now be equivalent to the walking dead: living forever but permanently separated from their Maker because of their sin, just like the fallen angels. Just like Satan.

Michael's Intervention

A spiritual truth is learned from Michael's intervention to aid God in delivering His message. God didn't need Michael. In fact, God doesn't need any of us to help Him carry out His will. But in His wisdom he chooses to partner both with us and with His angelic beings to accomplish His will.

So, when we say no to God, does that prevent Him from achieving His will? Unfortunately for us, He then partners with someone else to get it done. He values relationship with us, preferring to do things *with* His people rather than doing the same things entirely on His own.

Certainly, as most of us are aware, fallen angels (evil spirits, devils) can come against us to try to disrupt and prevent the work of God. But God doesn't want us partnering with them. The lesson here is that God wants to be our exclusive partner just as He was with Daniel.

And sometimes God wants us to persist in efforts to get His attention. Sometimes He wants to see just how serious we really are in pursuing Him, and/or His knowledge and wisdom. Twenty-one days can seem like a long time, especially when you're fasting. But what would have happened if Daniel had quit at day 20? Do we get impatient with God when we try to get clarity in our own lives? The lesson here is for us to press in, persevere, and know that God will bring His insights at His own appointed time.

Our behavior affects the workings within the spirit world, either for us or against us. Are there other things that we can do with respect to the spirit world around and about us that would give greater control (or authority) in our own lives? And, to positively affect the lives around us by influencing others with the light of God?

Of course the answer to both of these questions is a big yes. We see it in the parable of the talents in Matthew 25 and in the concepts of tithing, fasting, and praying as explained throughout the Bible. In Malachi it says to test God in this matter, to see if He won't pour out a blessing on those who obey Him.

How to Be Great in the Kingdom

There are way too many examples in the Bible to ignore the obvious fact that if you want to be great in the kingdom of God (i.e., to be given more authority), you must obey God.

The book of Job introduces a fellow who is called a blameless man (Job 1:1). God had put a hedge of protection around him because of his relationship and obedience to God. Satan wants to come and test this man of God, but before he is allowed to do so he has to get God to drop the "spheres of protection" that God had put around Job. How many spheres do you have around your own life, and who has put them there?

Job 1:8 calls Job "perfect, upright, and a man who fears God and departs from evil." Examining the original Hebrew words and their underlying meaning specifies that Job was upright and whole in a moral sense. He had integrity. He was "straight," metaphorically representing someone who does not deviate from the path of goodness.

Fearing God means that Job revered or feared God in the sense of having the proper respect. The Hebrew words that get interpreted as "departs from evil" mean that Job had turned away from choosing wrong paths, choosing instead pathways that received God's approval. These attributes and inclinations should be our goals as well.

In the passage below, God gives us specific information about Lucifer, or Satan. Various English translations use different names, but the Hebrew word for Lucifer is *Halal*, which doesn't mean Lucifer at all, but rather a "bright star" or "to shine."[2] The name Lucifer might have been derived from the Latin word for *light*, or *to shine* as in *lucent*. Thus the translators rendered the Hebrew word meaning "bright star," as "Lucifer."

> "How the oppressor has ceased,
> And how fury has ceased!
> [5] The LORD has broken the staff of the wicked,
> The scepter of rulers
> [6] Which used to strike the peoples in fury with unceasing strokes,
> Which subdued the nations in anger with unrestrained persecution.
> [7] The whole earth is at rest and is quiet;
> They break forth into shouts of joy.
> [8] Even the cypress trees rejoice over you, and the cedars of Lebanon, saying,
> 'Since you were laid low, no tree cutter comes up against us.'
> [9] Sheol from beneath is excited over you to meet you when you come;
> It arouses for you the spirits of the dead, all the leaders of the earth;
> It raises all the kings of the nations from their thrones.
> [10] They will all respond and say to you,
> 'Even you have been made weak as we,
> You have become like us.
> [11] Your pomp and the music of your harps
> Have been brought down to Sheol;
> Maggots are spread out as your bed beneath you
> And worms are your covering.'
> [12] How you have fallen from heaven,
> O star of the morning, son of the dawn!
> You have been cut down to the earth,
> You who have weakened the nations!
> [13] But you said in your heart,
> 'I will ascend to heaven;
> I will raise my throne above the stars of God,
> And I will sit on the mount of assembly

In the recesses of the north.
[14] I will ascend above the heights of the clouds;
I will make myself like the Most High.'
[15] Nevertheless you will be thrust down to Sheol,
To the recesses of the pit.
[16] Those who see you will gaze at you,
They will ponder over you, saying,
'Is this the man who made the earth tremble,
Who shook kingdoms,
[17] Who made the world like a wilderness
And overthrew its cities,
Who did not allow his prisoners to go home?'
[18] All the kings of the nations lie in glory,
Each in his own tomb.
[19] But you have been cast out of your tomb
Like a rejected branch,
Clothed with the slain who are pierced with a sword,
Who go down to the stones of the pit
Like a trampled corpse." (Isaiah 14:4–19)

This passage identifies a consistent theme that the devil wants to communicate to us – that he, rather than God, is the source of the light that should be guiding our pathways. We can see that his desire finds its source in pride, as in verses 13 and 14 when he repeats again and again "I will" rather than sourcing God's will.

In verse 13 we see him challenging the very creator God when he says, "I will ascend to heaven, and I will raise my throne above the stars of God, and I will sit on the mount." The text then continues to describe how Satan will exalt himself, even above the Most High God.

Unfortunately for Satan, Ezekiel 28:15 tells us that he is not God. He is a created being that started out as blameless in his ways. But things changed over the course of time, and the text tells us that evil was found in him and he was violent, and that he had sinned and become prideful.

The original Hebrew words imply that he had become wicked and filled with iniquity. The word for violence talks about being a false witness—in other words, being a liar—and pursuing gain by doing wrong. Obviously, Satan didn't fear God very much! Otherwise he wouldn't have been inhibited from doing what was right. The word *khatah*, a common Hebrew word for "sin," means to err, miss the mark, and to forfeit, [3] and certainly that is a description of the life of Lucifer. He is one who has missed the mark because he is purposely attempting to do what is evil in the eyes of God. He certainly, as well, has forfeited his life and replaced it with judgment to come.

It seems that this fallen cherub had become prideful; he was one of the most beautiful creatures and had great splendor. But those God-given gifts caused exactly the opposite of what God intended. Satan began to believe that he was the source of his own greatness and thereby corrupted himself.

Do we ever do similar things and think similar thoughts? Ask yourself these questions: Who do I depend on? Is it myself or do I rely on God to intervene on my behalf? Who is the source of my successes? Who is giving the direction for my life?

Is there a code that we should live by? And if so, for you, who is the source of this code? For Satan the source of that code was himself. He follows his own rules. But God's people must follow God's principles for holy living, exactly as Daniel did.

9

The Antichrist and His Archetype, Antiochus

(Daniel 11)

D aniel was fasting again. This time his fasting was for those who would have to deal with a coming tyrant — the one who was the subject of many of his dreams and visions. The man/beast that would come at the End of Days was truly something unique to all of mankind throughout the ages. Pride, arrogance, and a lust to rule the entire world, just like the real God would do, were his identifying traits.

But it didn't end there. He would possess one other unique quality. Daniel had been led to know, by his God, that this tyrant would be part man and part angel. The angelic part would be Satan himself, indwelling the body of a man in the final days, causing mankind to marvel and be inspired by him. Not realizing that they were being deceived into believing a lie, people would think that this "king" was actually doing much good.

In fact, this supposed peacemaker would proclaim himself to be God, and very few people would realize that it was all a ruse. He would even raise himself from the dead after receiving a fatal shot to the head, emulating Yeshua when He rose from the dead. His false prophet would call down fire from heaven, just like Elijah of old who — unlike this imposter — truly was a prophet of God. All of this would wow the earth's inhabitants.

One thing confounded Daniel. Why would this beast possess the body of a man? Why not just appear as all cherubim do — with six wings covered with feathers, having four faces, and standing about twice as tall as any mere human? That would certainly bring awe in the eyes of Satan's newfound worshipers. Why indwell a feeble man?

The answer came to King Nebuchadnezzar one day as Daniel and the king were discussing this very thing. During the king's seven-year experience as a beast he had lost his identity and authority, becoming nothing more than a wandering soul. The king's understanding was then confirmed by what Daniel's scriptures, called Torah, said in its very first few toledot in the book of Genesis.

At the fall in Eden, Satan lost his own identity and authority. The only identity and authority he had was what men gave him through their obedience and their allegiance to him. God had removed Satan's authority; he was no longer the covering angel. He used to be the one who was the master over covenant, leading men and women on a lighted pathway to greater and more intimate relationships with their Creator. Now he had no God-given authority of his own.

He also lost his identity. As Daniel had realized via so many encounters with angelic beings, all of the ones who worked for his God had names ending in "el," which means "God" in the Hebrew language. This was no coincidence. God had embedded within their very names who they really were. These angels had names that translated into English as Redemmer of God, Light of God, Healer of God, or other similar expressions that illuminated their identity and their purpose in the kingdom of God.

But the word "satan" is not really a name. Rather, it is a description that certainly represents no identity associated with the kingdom of God. The word simply means an "enemy" or an "adversary." That is what this fallen cherub was now — permanently separated from God because he had decided, because of his pride, that he wanted to be God. In the process he became God's enemy. Daniel wondered if men, too, became God's enemies when they preferred to rule their own lives, choosing to ignore God's ways.

Nebuchadnezzar's understanding was that Satan wanted to indwell a man because doing so allowed him to regain an identity and an authority: man's identity and authority, no less. These qualities would be recognized and respected in the kingdom of God because they had been handed out by YHWH Himself! What kind of an "in your face idea" was that?! Satan must think this would be a perfect way to outmaneuver and outsmart God.

Daniel now realized that mankind still had an authority and identity given to them by God. At the beginning God had given mankind the authority to manage His creation, and mankind was also given a very interesting and desirable identity. He was literally created in the image of God. These realities were exactly what man's adversary had been lusting for over the centuries.

Daniel understood that if the adversary included man in the making of this beastly mix with an angel, Satan might reach his goal by effectively stealing the authority and identity given to mankind. Then, with the authority stolen from mankind, he himself might rule the earth as God!

For a moment Daniel wondered if this might really make a difference. Could Satan really make a play like this and tie God's hands, allowing Satan to overturn God's plans? Of course not. These were delusional thoughts of the serpent as he wallowed in pride. What God gave away He could just as well take back any time He wanted to. And that is exactly what Daniel's visions and dreams foretold.

Daniel knew that this same authority and identity would ultimately, and for all time, become the property of YHWH's bride, and never the adversary's. But Daniel decided to continue fasting for the people who would live concurrently with that beast. They would need all the prayer and angelic help they could get.

Daniel 11:1–30 tells us:

> [1] "In the first year of Darius the Mede, I arose to be an encouragement and a protection for him. [2] And now I

will tell you the truth. Behold, three more kings are going to arise in Persia. Then a fourth will gain far more riches than all of them; as soon as he becomes strong through his riches, he will arouse the whole empire against the realm of Greece. [3] And a mighty king will arise, and he will rule with great authority and do as he pleases. [4] But as soon as he has arisen, his kingdom will be broken up and parceled out toward the four points of the compass, though not to his own descendants, nor according to his authority which he wielded, for his sovereignty will be uprooted and given to others besides them.

[5] "Then the king of the South will grow strong, along with one of his princes who will gain ascendancy over him and obtain dominion; his domain will be a great dominion indeed. [6] After some years they will form an alliance, and the daughter of the king of the South will come to the king of the North to carry out a peaceful arrangement. But she will not retain her position of power, nor will he remain with his power, but she will be given up, along with those who brought her in and the one who sired her as well as he who supported her in those times. [7] But one of the descendants of her line will arise in his place, and he will come against their army and enter the fortress of the king of the North, and he will deal with them and display great strength. [8] Also their gods with their metal images and their precious vessels of silver and gold he will take into captivity to Egypt, and he on his part will refrain from attacking the king of the North for some years. [9] Then the latter will enter the realm of the king of the South, but will return to his own land.

[10] "His sons will mobilize and assemble a multitude of great forces; and one of them will keep on coming and overflow and pass through, that he may again wage war up to his very fortress. [11] The king of the South will be enraged and go forth and fight with the king of the North. Then the latter will raise a great multitude, but that multitude will be

given into the hand of the former. [12] When the multitude is carried away, his heart will be lifted up, and he will cause tens of thousands to fall; yet he will not prevail. [13] For the king of the North will again raise a greater multitude than the former, and after an interval of some years he will press on with a great army and much equipment.

[14] "Now in those times many will rise up against the king of the South; the violent ones among your people will also lift themselves up in order to fulfill the vision, but they will fall down. [15] Then the king of the North will come, cast up a siege ramp and capture a well-fortified city; and the forces of the South will not stand their ground, not even their choicest troops, for there will be no strength to make a stand. [16] But he who comes against him will do as he pleases, and no one will be able to withstand him; he will also stay for a time in the Beautiful Land, with destruction in his hand. [17] He will set his face to come with the power of his whole kingdom, bringing with him a proposal of peace which he will put into effect; he will also give him the daughter of women to ruin it. But she will not take a stand for him or be on his side. [18] Then he will turn his face to the coastlands and capture many. But a commander will put a stop to his scorn against him; moreover, he will repay him for his scorn. [19] So he will turn his face toward the fortresses of his own land, but he will stumble and fall and be found no more.

[20] "Then in his place one will arise who will send an oppressor through the Jewel of his kingdom; yet within a few days he will be shattered, though not in anger nor in battle. [21] In his place a despicable person will arise, on whom the honor of kingship has not been conferred, but he will come in a time of tranquility and seize the kingdom by intrigue. [22] The overflowing forces will be flooded away before him and shattered, and also the prince of the covenant. [23] After an alliance is made with him he will practice deception,

and he will go up and gain power with a small force of people. [24] In a time of tranquility he will enter the richest parts of the realm, and he will accomplish what his fathers never did, nor his ancestors; he will distribute plunder, booty and possessions among them, and he will devise his schemes against strongholds, but only for a time. [25] He will stir up his strength and courage against the king of the South with a large army; so the king of the South will mobilize an extremely large and mighty army for war; but he will not stand, for schemes will be devised against him. [26] Those who eat his choice food will destroy him, and his army will overflow, but many will fall down slain. [27] As for both kings, their hearts will be intent on evil, and they will speak lies to each other at the same table; but it will not succeed, for the end is still to come at the appointed time. [28] Then he will return to his land with much plunder; but his heart will be set against the holy covenant, and he will take action and then return to his own land.

[29] "At the appointed time he will return and come into the South, but this last time it will not turn out the way it did before. [30] For ships of Kittim will come against him; therefore he will be disheartened and will return and become enraged at the holy covenant and take action; so he will come back and show regard for those who forsake the holy covenant."

Another reason the book of Daniel is purported to be a fraud, and written not in the 6th century BC but in the last century BC or first century AD, depending on the speculator, is because of the above text. It is too much for these prognosticators to propose that Daniel could have actually received a prophecy that came true in the following five centuries. So, they moved the date of the writing of Daniel's book up by five or six hundred years and claimed that its author was not Daniel but had to be someone else – some imposter. In so doing they eliminated the seemingly miraculous nature of the fulfillment of parts of Daniel's text.

As we have already discovered, many substantial archeological finds have been made over the last century. These have established that the book of Daniel was indeed written sometime during the 6th century BC, while Daniel was actually in exile in Babylon. Most, if not all, of the above prophecy, in chapter 11, has been fulfilled. As we have learned so far, during the time that this vision was given, the ruler of Persia was Cyrus, who had appointed Darius to be governor over the province of Babylon.

Daniel 11:2 refers to three additional kings that shall come after Cyrus, with the one who follows these three having great wealth. These three kings were Cambyses, the son of Cyrus, 530-522 BC; Smerdis, an imposter who impersonated the real Smerdis, 522 BC; and Darius I, 522-487 BC. The fourth ruler is the one most familiar: Xerxes (Ahasuerus) who was married to Queen Esther. And she, of course, is lovingly remembered at Purim for risking her life to save her fellow Jews. Xerxes is well known for amassing an army approaching six million warriors with which he attacked the area that became Greece.

Daniel 11:3 speaks of a mighty king that shall stand up, shall have great dominion, and shall do everything he wants. This passage introduces us to the next kingdom.

The Kingdom of Greece

Just as Daniel had prophesied 200 years before Alexander was born, after Alexander's sudden death his kingdom was divided into four regions by four of his generals. Those four were Seleucus, Ptolemy, Lysimachus, and Cassander. Two of these generals became prominent, and that ascendance dominates Daniel's prophecy from this point on. The text tells us Seleucus became the king of the North, and Ptolemy became the king of the South.

Daniel 11 has multiple references to the king of the North and the king of the South. Most of the time Daniel's references to the king of the North denote the Seleucid Empire. This empire included what are now Syria, Lebanon, and Iraq, plus regions north.

The empire of the king of the South, Ptolemy, included Egypt and other parts of North Africa that Alexander had conquered. Israel was stuck right in the middle between these two significant regional powers, which were constantly fighting each other and using Israel as their battlefield.

Daniel 11:6 speaks of an arranged marriage intended to make peace between these two empires. In what reads as the Peyton Place of the Greek Empire, Berenice's father, Ptolemy Philadelphus (285-247 BC), died when the king of the North, Antiochus, threw Bernice out of his court and remarried his ex-wife. In the process, Bernice, the daughter of the Ptolemic king, was killed. The ex-wife, Laodice, remarried the king, and then poisoned him and had Callinicus pronounced king in Antiochus's place.

In reading on from verse 6 we find that there was much intrigue, political maneuvering, and many wars between these two kingdoms, all of which affected the people of Israel.

And this particular King Antiochus, murdered by Laodice, was one of a long line of Antiochuses who ruled the Seleucid Empire to the north of Israel.

Introduction to Antiochus

The king we want to give the most attention to is the one Daniel dealt with in his prophetic writings. Starting in Daniel 8:23 we are introduced to Antiochus Epiphanes, who lived from 215 to 164 BC and ruled the Seleucid Empire from 175 to 164 BC[1]. He expanded the empire and finally conquered all of Israel, plus large portions of Egypt. His life should be thoroughly studied by all of those who want to know more about the end-times false messiah, or antichrist, for this Antiochus is an archetype. By studying his life and his accomplishments we can see a mirror image of the false messiah.

> [28] "Then he will return to his land with much plunder; but his heart will be set against the holy covenant, and he will take action and then return to his own land.

[29] "At the appointed time he will return and come into the South, but this last time it will not turn out the way it did before. [30] For ships of Kittim will come against him; therefore he will be disheartened and will return and become enraged at the holy covenant and take action; so he will come back and show regard for those who forsake the holy covenant.

[31] "Forces from him will arise, desecrate the sanctuary fortress, and do away with the regular sacrifice. And they will set up the abomination of desolation. [32] By smooth words he will turn to godlessness those who act wickedly toward the covenant, but the people who know their God will display strength and take action. [33] Those who have insight among the people will give understanding to the many; yet they will fall by sword and by flame, by captivity and by plunder for many days. [34] Now when they fall they will be granted a little help, and many will join with them in hypocrisy. [35] Some of those who have insight will fall, in order to refine, purge and make them pure until the end time; because it is still to come at the appointed time.

[36] "Then the king will do as he pleases, and he will exalt and magnify himself above every god and will speak monstrous things against the God of gods; and he will prosper until the indignation is finished, for that which is decreed will be done. [37] He will show no regard for the gods of his fathers or for the desire of women, nor will he show regard for any other god; for he will magnify himself above them all. [38] But instead he will honor a god of fortresses, a god whom his fathers did not know; he will honor him with gold, silver, costly stones and treasures. [39] He will take action against the strongest of fortresses with the help of a foreign god; he will give great honor to those who acknowledge him and will cause them to rule over the many, and will parcel out land for a price.

[40] "At the end time the king of the South will collide with him, and the king of the North will storm against him with chariots, with horsemen and with many ships; and he will enter countries, overflow them and pass through. [41] He will also enter the Beautiful Land, and many countries will fall; but these will be rescued out of his hand: Edom, Moab and the foremost of the sons of Ammon. [42] Then he will stretch out his hand against other countries, and the land of Egypt will not escape. [43] But he will gain control over the hidden treasures of gold and silver and over all the precious things of Egypt; and Libyans and Ethiopians will follow at his heels. [44] But rumors from the East and from the North will disturb him, and he will go forth with great wrath to destroy and annihilate many. [45] He will pitch the tents of his royal pavilion between the seas and the beautiful Holy Mountain; yet he will come to his end, and no one will help him." (Daniel 11:28–45)

The above section of text focuses on Antiochus Epiphanes. From it we learn that when he conquered Israel he desecrated the temple and forced Hellenism on the Israelites. Hellenism was a perverse religion that worshipped the human body and sexual and moral perversions of every sort, all of which were integral parts of the Greek culture of that era.

To give us a little insight into the state of mind of Antiochus, he added "Epiphanes" to his name, which means "God made manifest." Of course he wasn't God made manifest, and the Jews immediately made fun of him by calling him Antiochus *Epimanes*, which means *madman*.

In his zeal to impose his own cultural norm upon Israel he built gymnasiums for the purpose of entertaining the population with nude athletic competition. He passed a law banning the study of Torah and the application of many of its principles, such as circumcision. Anyone found violating his changes to the law was slaughtered. He was known to crucify many women because they had circumcised their male children. He would tie the woman's child around her neck while crucifying her on a cross.

The king also put the position of high priest up for bid instead of going to members of the Zadokean line exclusively. Zadok was a descendant of Aaron. God had given Aaron and his descendants the responsibility to be the high priest serving in the temple of God.

Bidding for a Position

The winners of the bidding war for the position of high priest eventually became the Sadducean group, which controlled the temple and its workings during Yeshua's lifetime. The Sadducees were largely descendants from Aaron, but not exclusively. The Hassidim formed a group of Jewish religious leaders who opposed all of the perversions brought on by Sadducees. The Hassidim eventually became the Pharisees that we read about in the New Testament.

The famous cliché, "Don't cross this line," used today when threatening someone, comes from a confrontation between Antiochus Epiphanes and Popilius Laenas, one of the commanders of Rome, who had taken positions against Antiochus in Alexandria, Egypt. The Roman commander, when confronting Antiochus and trying to prevent him from taking the city, drew a circle around Antiochus and said, "You have to make a decision as to what you're going to do before you cross this line," preventing the king from getting advice from his counselors. As history records, Antiochus backed down, which made this a major turning point in establishing the growing power that Rome eventually acquired.

An interesting thing about the last half of Daniel 11 is that it includes a subtle transition from prophesying about Antiochus to prophesying about the end-time false messiah. However, it is somewhat difficult to tell exactly where the transition occurs. More than likely Daniel is actually talking about both of them, because both of them will do many of the same things in the end. Remember, Antiochus Epiphanes is an archetype of the false messiah who is yet to come.

The exploits of these two are perfectly described in verse 36. To paraphrase, they both magnified themselves above God Himself and spoke monstrous things against Him. The prophecy includes information about the people of God and how they opposed Antiochus Epiphanes, just as the people of God will oppose the false messiah yet to come. Even so, many will fall, either physically or spiritually. But God says that the purpose of this testing is to purge them and make them pure (Daniel 11:35).

Some propose that verse 37 is suggesting that this beast will be a homosexual. And current teachers who maintain that the Bible prophesies that gold and silver will lose their value in the last days are clearly wrong, by virtue of what's recorded in verse 38. This man is supposed to be a man of war even though he will endeavor to sell the idea that he is a man of peace. He will attempt to conquer the entire world.

The final verse of this chapter is intriguing inasmuch as it prophesies that this beast and his army will have their end. It says that the beast's end will come between the seas and the beautiful holy mountain. A reference to seas in the Bible usually refers to the Dead Sea and the Mediterranean Sea. And the holy mountain is Mount Zion, where the temple will reside. So, somewhere south of Jerusalem, between those two seas, is where the false messiah and his army will get their just reward.

The sixth bowl in Revelation 16:12 dries up the Euphrates River, making the way possible for the kings of the east to gather for war. Daniel 11:44 mentions that this beast will be disturbed by rumors about news from the East and from the North. Are these two verses talking about the same thing – Armageddon, in which all the armies of the world come together for one last battle?

What can we conclude about this false messiah and his archetype, Antiochus Epiphanes? We know that they will desecrate the temple in Jerusalem, and that they will both claim to be God. As Antiochus gained power by flattery and intrigue, might not the antichrist do the same? And, we've learned that all those who don't conform to the wiles of these evil rulers, such as God's people, will be made targets for persecution. At the same time, some people propose that we don't have to worry about the end times because we will all be raptured up before this beast, the false messiah, ever shows his face and makes his move on the temple.

Unfortunately, the biblical text does not line up with that view. II Thessalonians 2:3–4 makes it clear that there will be two great signs before the coming of God for His people. The first one will be a great falling away, in contrast to what many hope will be a great revival. The second sign, as prophesied by Paul, is that just before the coming of our Lord we will see the abomination of the temple, soon followed by God's return for His people. This will require patient endurance, trusting, and reliance upon God. Otherwise, you too might be counted among those who fall away from the truth.

Just as Antiochus did when he brought deception to so many people, so also will the beast do. Those who will be able to stand through these perverse lies will be ones who know their God and have a strong relationship with Him.

10

The Final Beast
(Daniel 12)

O h, how lovely those gardens were – the ones Daniel admired through his window. He was very appreciative that he could see such beauty without leaving his home as, more and more, it became difficult to walk. He had help picking up food and other things he needed. Joshua, the son of his old friend Jehozadak, would come twice a week to check up on him and pick up anything the old prophet might need.

Remember that smelly camel Daniel was tied to as he was led to his new home in Babylon, being newly exiled from Jerusalem? Jehozadak, in the lineage to be high priest, was also tied to that same camel. They had known each other before the exile, having once taken some of the same study courses in preparation for serving God and His people. But while tied to that camel they had become really good friends and maintained that friendship through all the years in exile. That is how Daniel knew Joshua. In keeping with God's instructions, Joshua was in line to become the next high priest, if only there was a temple to serve in.

Daniel was a great source of inspiration and hope to the young man. When Joshua would come by with all the supplies on the list, Daniel would tell him stories and explain prophecies in the Scriptures about how the temple would be rebuilt. And the best part was about the passage in Jeremiah that foretold that the end of this time of exile was coming soon. The people of God were going home. As Daniel told those stories he knew that the part about going back to Jerusalem didn't include him. But the part about going home did. He knew that his God would always take care of him, even after he died. Daniel had nothing to worry about ever again.

Even so, one of Daniel's greatest concerns as he looked out his window was how to make sure that his scroll, which contained all of these end-time messages, would be preserved. At that very moment there came a knock on the outside wall. It was an immediate answer to how he would ensure preservation of his precious dreams and visions.

Joshua! He would certainly be one of those who would return to their homeland and could take Daniel's writings back to Jerusalem where they could be properly preserved. Daniel knew that the Jewish scribes were experts at creating exact copies and maintaining ancient texts for future generations to read. That is what they had done in preserving for the world the very words that God spoke to Moses on Mount Sinai nine hundred years previously.

Daniel couldn't know for sure that Joshua would indeed go back to Jerusalem and become the first high priest after the Babylonian exile. But God did. This young man, who stood before him now holding the makings of this evening's meal, would be followed by Ezra who would help restore the temple in Jerusalem. And indeed, Daniel's words truly would be preserved for all time.

———

Because Daniel 12 is the last of Daniel's seven prophecies, you would expect it to bring the age of man and the culmination of God's work to an end. And that's exactly what it does.

Recall that this last prophecy is actually the second phase of a much larger prophecy which started in Daniel 10. The same being who delivered that prophecy is here in Daniel 12. This being was not an angel. Revelation 1:13–16 and 2:18 describe the Messiah the same way Daniel describes Him:

> [5] I lifted my eyes and looked, and behold, there was a certain man dressed in linen, whose waist was girded with a belt of pure gold of Uphaz. [6] His body also was like beryl, his face had the appearance of lightning, his eyes were like flaming torches, his arms and feet like the gleam of polished bronze, and the sound of his words like the sound of a tumult. [7] Now I, Daniel, alone saw the vision, while the men who were with me did not see the vision; nevertheless, a great dread fell on them, and they ran away to hide themselves. (Daniel 10:5-7)

The man in linen is still above the Tigris River in Daniel 12:7 but has both hands raised toward heaven, swearing by God (Elohim, who lives forever and ever) as he gives pronouncements about the end times.

As we concluded, this man was very likely the Messiah. Here we see Him acting as a priest, with both hands raised up as if to speak for God and bring blessing or judgment as a priest would. If you're a Star Trek fan, you can picture how Spock would greet or bless people by holding up his hand and grouping his fingers to form a W, with two fingers on each side and the thumb spread apart. This forms the Hebrew letter *shin*, which looks like our W. The priest would hold up both hands, connecting the thumbs and forefingers, and bless the people. One of the blessings that he would say would be what we know as the Aaronic blessing:

> [24] "The Lord bless you, and keep you; [25] The Lord make His face shine on you, And be gracious to you; [26] The Lord lift up His countenance on you, And give you peace." (Numbers 6:24–26)

In many Jewish and messianic congregations today, the rabbis at the end of the service do likewise, following the instruction that God gave Moses some 3,500 years ago. Here we see the Messiah doing a similar thing, except that He is bringing additional instructions to Daniel that will see their fulfillment at the end of time.

In Daniel 12 He is acting as a priest, with both hands raised, but in Revelation 10 this same being comes down from heaven holding a scroll. This is the same entity and the same scroll that appeared in Revelation 5 – the scroll that no one was found worthy to open except Himself. And He's clearly identified there as the Messiah, for He is described as the one who died but lives again. In Revelation 10 we see this being (the Messiah), once again appearing with the same scroll in His hand. But now it's open.

John is witnessing the events of the book of Revelation approximately sixty years after the death and resurrection of this same Messiah. Revelation 10 describes the Messiah holding a scroll, but swearing by God with only his right hand raised. This form of making proclamations, or blessings, symbolizes how a king would do it.

The question then arises: Why does He act as a priest one time, then another time as the king? All throughout Israel's history God wanted those two positions of authority to be separated. The Israelites violated those instructions from time to time, but for the most part they honored what God wanted. The reason for God's mandate was that only one special being was to ever act in the capacity of the king and the high priest at the same time, and that was God Himself.

This is why the genealogy of Yeshua comes down from King David's bloodline on both His mother and father's sides, but he also became the high priest forever according to the order of Melchizedek (Hebrews 6:20). In other words, the priestly line would come from Melchizedek and the kingly line would come through the kingly tribe of Judah. This is exactly what Yeshua's position as God's Son and His human bloodline accomplished. In the vision in Daniel 12, our Messiah could only act as our priest. He had not won the authority over sin and death yet to act as our king.

But in Revelation 10:5 we see our king raising His hand, representing this new authority. The seventh trumpet blasts in Revelation 11, showing that the kingdom of this world has become the kingdom of our Lord.

> Then the seventh angel sounded; and there were loud voices in heaven, saying, "The kingdom of the world has become the kingdom of our Lord and of His Christ; and He will reign forever and ever." (Revelation 11:15)

In the above passage we see our Messiah taking up those reins of authority and acting as the King that He truly is.

Michael and the Final Judgment

As we've noted, this angelic being, whom we believe is the Messiah, is described in Daniel 12:6. But the first five verses of this chapter are actually completing the prophecy that started in chapter 10. Recall that the chapter and verse designations were inserted into the text by man, to help in referencing certain passages. In this case it might have been better to start chapter 12 at verse 6. Nonetheless, the first five verses of Daniel 12 describe another being, the great prince Michael who will stand up and protect God's people during these last few years.

> [1] "Now at that time Michael, the great prince who stands guard over the sons of your people, will arise. And there will be a time of distress such as never occurred since there was a nation until that time; and at that time your people, everyone who is found written in the book, will be rescued. [2] Many of those who sleep in the dust of the ground will awake, these to everlasting life, but the others to disgrace and everlasting contempt. [3] Those who have insight will shine brightly like the brightness of the expanse of heaven, and those who lead the many to righteousness, like the stars forever and ever. [4] But as for you, Daniel, conceal these words and seal up the book until the end of time; many will go back and forth, and knowledge will increase." [5] Then I, Daniel, looked and behold, two others were standing, one on this bank of the river and the other on that bank of the river. (Daniel 12:1–5)

These verses describe a period of time in which there will be the worst distress ever visited upon mankind. It mentions the Book of Life, and how those who are found in it will be rescued. It also talks about some being resurrected to everlasting life, while others are being resurrected to everlasting contempt.

The Hebrew word translated as contempt is *deraon*. In Hebrew that word actually means "abhorrent, abomination."[1] This word is used only one other time in the Bible, in the last verse of Isaiah:

> "Then they will go forth and look
> On the corpses of the men
> Who have transgressed against Me.
> For their worm will not die
> And their fire will not be quenched;
> And they will be an abhorrence [*deraon*] to all mankind."
> (Isaiah 66:24)

Here, Isaiah is prophesying about how God, at the final judgment, will punish men for their transgressions against Him. Their ultimate judgment will be the fire that cannot be quenched, and they will be perceived by the rest of mankind as an abomination and an abhorrence to others. This lines up perfectly with what Daniel is saying in our passage in chapter 12. What will those people think when they realize that they are an everlasting abomination to their Creator and their name is not found in the Book of Life?

I would rather be on the side of Michael, a great prince who is coming to protect God's people. In Revelation the Book of Life is referenced seven times, two of which are found in Revelation 20:12–15:

> [12] And I saw the dead, the great and the small, standing before the throne, and books were opened; and another book was opened, which is the book of life; and the dead were judged from the things which were written in the books, according to their deeds. [13] And the sea gave up the dead which were in it, and death and Hades gave up the dead which were in them; and they were judged, every one of them according to their deeds. [14] Then death and Hades were thrown into the lake of fire. This is the second death,

the lake of fire. [15] And if anyone's name was not found written in the book of life, he was thrown into the lake of fire.

This passage confirms the judgment that other prophets in the Bible have also predicted. John refers to this judgment as the second death and prophesies that those who get judged in this manner are abhorrent, are an abomination to God, and will be thrown into the lake of fire. And he describes them as *not* having their names found in the Book of Life.

Daniel 12:3 refers to the wise and predicts a blessing upon them. The Hebrew word *sakal,* most often interpreted as "wise," means "to be prudent," "to be attentive," and "to turn the mind to."[2] So what will these wise folks be attentive to and watching so closely? It's the very thing that makes them shine as brightly as stars in this passage – they will know and apply the truths found in the Bible.

Daniel 12:4 predicts that knowledge will increase in the time of the end. Daniel is told that the words he's been given are sealed up until that time. Certainly the prophecy of increased knowledge has been fulfilled by mankind's progress in computer technology which has allowed, through the internet, information to be accessible like never before. But we believe that the knowledge Daniel is referring to is also inclusive of the increase in knowledge of the truth about God. The word for knowledge here is *daat*, which means "knowledge, understanding, wisdom"[3], and the pictography of the word shows that wisdom and knowledge comprise the pathway that leads to the sign of the covenant. This, then, implies that the more you study God's Word the more it leads to a closer relationship with Him.

The Beginning of the End . . . Times

[8] As for me, I heard but could not understand; so I said, "My lord, what will be the outcome of these events?" [9] He said, "Go your way, Daniel, for these words are concealed and sealed up until the end time. [10] Many will be purged, purified and refined, but the wicked will act wickedly; and none of the wicked will understand, but those who have

insight will understand. [11] From the time that the regular sacrifice is abolished and the abomination of desolation is set up, there will be 1,290 days. [12] How blessed is he who keeps waiting and attains to the 1,335 days! [13] But as for you, go your way to the end; then you will enter into rest and rise again for your allotted portion at the end of the age." (Daniel 12:8–13)

The last week of Daniel's seventy-week prophecy will last seven years. These seven years follow the 49-year period which began with the proclamation to rebuild Jerusalem. We have learned that this 49-year period started in 1967 and terminates in the year 2015. In Revelation 12, the first half of this last seven years is referred to as "time, times, and half a time" and describes a period of persecution of God's people at the hand of the beast.

God steps forward to protect His people by preparing a place in the wilderness for them. This time period is also described in Daniel 12:1. Michael, the archangel, the great prince who guards over God's called-out ones, will protect God's people from a great time of distress. In fact, the distress is so great that its severity has never before been seen on the earth. We're told that during these times of judgment many will be tested, some will be found wanting, and others will be refined and purified. This will be a time of great confusion.

Sometime near the end of this first 3-1/2 years, the sixth trumpet is blown, marking the time of the Gog/Magog war when Russia attacks Israel (Ezekiel 38, 39; Revelation 9:13–19). At the same time, or at the concluding days of this war, the two witnesses are given authority (Revelation 11:3). The time of the two witnesses also encompasses the time of the kingdom of the beast as described in Revelation 13. This period equates to the last 3-1/2 years of Daniel's 70-week prophecy. The temple sacrifices are stopped, initiating the beginning of this period (Daniel 12:11). The two witnesses are killed by the beast at the end of the 3-1/2 year period. But so too ends the beast's kingdom and his authority to reign over the earth.

At the completion of the 70 weeks of Daniel, Revelation 11:15 informs us that "The kingdom of the world has become the kingdom of our Lord and of His Christ; and He will reign forever and ever." Daniel says the end of the 70-week prophecy brings in everlasting righteousness (Daniel 9:24).

Most students of the Bible believe that what occurs next is the beginning of the thousand year reign, and I would agree. However, the common idea of peace and calm settling over the earth's landscapes is not what the biblical text seems to be describing. What follows in Revelation is the seven bowls of judgment in chapter 16. These horrific curses are poured out upon those who have the mark of the beast and upon what remains of the beast's kingdom. God is purifying the earth as He sets up His reign. Daniel 12:12 tells us this period of purification lasts 1,335 days.

Being Set Apart: Old and New Testament

In contrast to those people who will be judged (those not found in the Book of Life), Daniel 12:7 highlights a holy people who are believers in God. The word "holy" here is *kodesh*. It means to be holy but also carries with it the idea of being set apart. The concept of being set apart is the fundamental foundational meaning for what constitutes God's people.

In the Old Testament, God's people are called *kehelot* which means "to be called out from amongst the people of the world," and that's what He called the congregation of Israel to be. He referred to them as those who were called out, those who were set apart for holy service. In the New Testament this concept is carried forward in the Greek word *ekklesia*. This Greek word maintains the same idea of a gathering of people who are called out, an assembly, or a congregation of people who are set apart from others.

Unfortunately, the translators did a great disservice by interpreting the Greek word *ekklesia* as "church," giving the impression that God is creating something new in the New Testament. This contrast comes from an inconsistency in translation. In actuality, God was very consistent. He continually defines His people as those who are called out, those who choose to separate themselves, morally and behaviorally, from the rest of the world and, in so doing, become lights for the lost. The last thing He is trying to do is give the idea that He's starting an entirely new and different assembly of people with a new religion.

The word "church" does not have biblical origins but is actually based on words from ancient Babylon, via the German language. The German word for church is *kirke*, which traces its roots back to Circe, an ancient pagan god and a Babylonian religious rite in which the pagans would stand in circles worshipping their pagan gods. We're not saying that people who use the word *church* are worshipping as pagans, but it is one of the reasons why Messianic congregations call themselves Messianic congregations rather than churches.

In Review

From the time when the regular sacrifice is abolished and the abomination of desolation is set up, there will be a 1,290 days (Daniel 12:11). In the middle of the last 7-year period, a covenant will be broken which was established 3-1/2 years earlier. At that point the false messiah will sit on the throne of the temple in Jerusalem, thereby bringing on the abomination of desolation at the same time the covenant is broken – in the middle of the last 7-years (Daniel 9:27).

Daniel 12:11 informs us that the regular sacrifice is abolished which initiates this 1,290-day period. Of course, in order for the daily sacrifice to be abolished it has to be reinstituted first, requiring a tabernacle, if not a temple, constructed on the Temple Mount in Jerusalem. This is one of the reasons we know God won't come tomorrow – because there is no temple on the Mount. In fact, the Dome of the Rock – a Muslim mosque – is standing on the Mount at this time.

Paul embellishes what we are saying in II Thessalonians when he relays to the Thessalonians the signs leading up to the Messiah's coming to gather His people to Himself.

> ¹ Now we request you, brethren, with regard to the coming of our Lord Jesus Christ and our gathering together to Him, ² that you not be quickly shaken from your composure or be disturbed either by a spirit or a message or a letter as if from us, to the effect that the day of the Lord has come. ³ Let no one in any way deceive you, for it will not come unless the apostasy comes first, and the man of lawlessness is revealed, the son of destruction, ⁴ who opposes and exalts himself above every so-called god or object of worship, so that he takes his seat in the temple of God, displaying himself as being God. (II Thessalonians 2:1–4)

The passage describes the lawless one as a son of destruction and details how he will be revealed. It describes him as a man who opposes and exalts himself above God and takes God's own seat in the temple, claiming to be God Himself. Given all those who claim that the Law, or Torah, has been abolished, it is interesting that the clues Paul gives to define the false messiah involve the Law. This beast, the one who opposed God in every way and the one for which the church has had its eyes peeled for ages, is said to be a lawless one.

The word translated as lawless is *anomos*. In Greek, when you put an "a" in front of a word, it's the equivalent of saying "without" or "no." In fact, the English language sometimes does the same thing: symmetric and asymmetric, for example. As we know, things that are symmetrical have sides or halves that are the same. But, by adding the "a" in front of "symmetric," the idea is communicated that the item in question is no longer symmetrical.

Nomos, from the Septuagint, is the equivalent Greek word for the Hebrew word *Torah*. So, anomos communicates that this person is anti-Torah, or against the laws of God. My question then, is: if the Law has been abolished by the work of Jesus on the cross, as many believers contend, how can it be a sign that this person will be the reprobate that we all know he is?

Daniel 12:12 adds even more information about these last few years when it says that the person who waits and persists for 1,335 days will be blessed. One way of interpreting this would be that these extra 45 days are added onto the 1,290 days spoken about in the previous verse. An alternate interpretation would be that these two numbers are linear and form a period that lasts 2,625 days with 1,335 days extending beyond the end of the last week in Daniel 9.

What Happens to God's People?

In Revelation 12:14, God protects His people, metaphorically being referred to as a woman, from the presence of the serpent for a time, times, and half a time. The serpent here is pictured as a red dragon, obviously referring to Satan, who later is personified as the antichrist, the beast who will bring abomination to the temple and will claim to be God.

> And she gave birth to a son, a male child, who is to rule all the nations with a rod of iron; and her child was caught up to God and to His throne. [6] Then the woman fled into the wilderness where she had a place prepared by God, so that there she would be nourished for one thousand two hundred and sixty days. [7] And there was war in heaven, Michael and his angels waging war with the dragon. The dragon and his angels waged war, [8] and they were not strong enough, and there was no longer a place found for them in heaven. (Revelation 12:5–8)

After God protects His people for 1,260 days, the beast rises up, abominates the temple, speaks blasphemous and arrogant words against the God in heaven, and is allowed to do this for 42 months (Revelation 13:5).

This 42-month period does not necessarily start at the same time that the 1,290-day period starts, described in Daniel 12:11. Nor do they end at the same time. But they do represent basically the same times.

In Revelation 13:7, during this 42-month period, the saints are completely overcome through continual confrontations and battles coming against them from the beast. This correlates nicely with the passage in

Daniel 12:7, which says that this 3-1/2-year period will be finished at the shattering of the power of the holy people. The collapse of influence of God's holy people on the earth will finish this time, times, and half-a-time period. It will also terminate a period lasting generally for 42 months (Revelation 13:5), but more specifically for 1,290 days as given in Daniel 12:11.

The Final Verse

The final verse in the book of Daniel is a message to Daniel, not to us. Daniel is instructed to "go your way and enter into your rest," referring to Daniel's death. The insinuation is that Daniel doesn't have to understand the intricacies of the end-time prophecies because they're not applicable to him.

That is not the message to our generation. God spent much time, giving much detail, for a definite reason. And that is so that we wouldn't be caught off guard. God wants us to be students of His Word so that we will identify the times we live in. Thus the implication is that it wasn't applicable to Daniel, but it is applicable to us.

11

Prophetic Signs in Our Times

B efore I begin the actual conclusion of this study of the book of Daniel, I want to emphasize something that you are probably aware of to some extent, but which I believe is of critical importance. The two biblical books that provide the clearest and most complete explanation of what's ahead, what most biblical scholars call the "end times," are the books of Daniel and Revelation. What is especially significant is that these two books absolutely *confirm* and *help explain* the events prophesied in each other.

This suggests rather strongly that God Himself was involved in the writing of each book. He purposely "worked out" the details in each one so that students of the Bible would be able to discern what He clearly wanted us to understand. Therefore, much of what I want to say in this conclusion will reflect on what has been learned from both Revelation and Daniel, which work together like two complementary halves of the same "story" — if we may call it that — to inform all of us. And, to help prepare those living today for what lies ahead.

That said, let's now look at Daniel, Revelation, and other signs together . . .

Astronomical Signs ARE from God!

Many people today are fascinated with the astrological phenomenon known as the four "blood moons" which are occurring in 2014 and 2015. We'll go into greater detail in a few more pages, but our point right here is that we all should be more sensitive to the signs that are unfolding before our very eyes.

This is true not only because of their spectacular nighttime display but also because of their rarity. And perhaps most significant of all, other biblical predictions seem to be coming true at the same time, all of which are pointing to the soon arrival of Daniel's God, YHWH. I hope you have made Him your God too. Time is running short, and sometime quite soon it might be too late to make that decision.

Daniel gave our generation — which is probably the last generation — many tools to use to identify these end times and this coming beast that he was so concerned about. Also, he gave us excellent detailed information that should alert all of us to the important events that will lead to the coming of our Messiah. Let's take a closer look at this information and see how it might harmonize with the four-blood-moon phenomenon. Remember, God told us that He would use the stars, moon, and sun as portents. He would use them to give us special, important warnings of things to come.

> Then God said, "Let there be lights in the expanse of the heavens to separate the day from the night, and let them be for signs and for seasons and for days and years." (Genesis 1:14)

The Hebrew word used above for signs is *ot*. It means a sign of something that is going to happen in the future; a portent or a prophecy[1]. There are those who say that any message coming from the stars must be associated with Satan and should be completely ignored because it's coming from an evil source. But is that really true? Certainly, messages coming from astrology are of the kingdom of darkness, but do the heavens make any other proclamations that may come from God?

In another one of our books, *Anatomy of the Heavens: God's Message in the Stars*[2], we showed that God originally created the heavenly bodies to speak messages to mankind. That Satan copied the idea does not make null and void God's messages. If God is really sending us signals, do these lunar and solar events represent His attempt to get our attention about things in our immediate future? We think so. It is the evil servant who is too shortsighted to prepare for His return.

> [44] "For this reason you also must be ready; for the Son of Man is coming at an hour when you do not think He will. [45] Who then is the faithful and sensible slave whom his master put in charge of his household to give them their food at the proper time? [46] Blessed is that slave whom his master finds so doing when he comes. [47] Truly I say to you that he will put him in charge of all his possessions. [48] But if that evil slave says in his heart, 'My master is not coming for a long time,' [49] and begins to beat his fellow slaves and eat and drink with drunkards, [50] the master of that slave will come on a day when he does not expect him and at an hour which he does not know, [51] and will cut him in pieces and assign him a place with the hypocrites; in that place there will be weeping and gnashing of teeth." (Matthew 24:44–51)

Are We Paying Attention?

Unfortunately, the evil servant in Matthew wasn't paying attention, and many in our generation might also be doing the same. Many people are just ignorant, but others don't really care. They seem to be swept up in the cares of their own lives, constantly wrestling with their personal hopes and dreams for accomplishments in this life. Thus they aren't paying attention to the warnings coming from God; they have become numb to His voice. They have their reasons – "good" reasons – in their own minds, anyway.

We seem to be inundated with end-time prophecies of late. To prove my point, just try googling the word "prophecy." So many of the examples that are supposedly coming from God, are not. They never seem to come true even though they are delivered with such certainty. Thus many predicted dates for various events come and go with no evidence of their fulfillment. No wonder people get tired of hearing this mush. But unfortunately, many of these *false* words cloud over the fact that there are some words that are *true*, coming from believers today and from the Bible as well.

Sometimes modern pastors add to the problem by pronouncements that we should not try to figure out the timing of God's return. Often they quote Matthew 24:36, "But of that day and hour no one knows, not even the angels of heaven, nor the Son, but the Father alone." They then use that verse to say, "See, we can never even learn about when He is coming. So stop it already!"

But that passage is not prohibiting the study of biblical prophecy. On the contrary, it is really giving us a clue as to when He will come back. Let's look at what Matthew might actually be saying.

Two thousand years ago the Feast of Trumpets was called "The Day and the Hour That No Man knows." This was because the exact day on which this feast occurred in any given year could not be determined ahead of time. It was the only festival that started on a new moon, and in ancient Israel each new moon was identified by the sighting of the new crescent by two credible witnesses. The state of astrological calculations in those days could only narrow the new moon sighting down to one of two days. And so the Feast of Trumpets became known as "The Day and the Hour That No Man Knows." Therefore, the Matthew text quoted above could actually be saying that the Messiah's coming might occur on a future Feast of Trumpets, not that we should not be attentive and study the signs.

As confirmation that God really wants us to be watching for the time of His return, recall Yeshua's reaction to those He confronted during His life here on earth. It really bothered Him that many in Israel were not informed of His coming and that they had not been given the tools by their leaders to know when it would happen.

What was Yeshua referring to? What were these religious leaders missing? We have learned that they had been given the keys to calculate His first coming in the book of Daniel. But, they were completely ignorant of the signs specifically written for them to see and use. Yeshua was angry with these leaders who should have known how to apply His Word. Instead, they did the same thing that some pastors do today. Modern pastors do not study the ancient Hebrew culture carefully enough to learn what such warnings actually mean, and neither do the people who listen to them: their flocks.

What would you do if you actually knew that God was coming back, say, next week on Saturday, on Shabbat? Would you do anything differently in the days leading up to that moment? Maybe a bit of house cleaning and repentance? Well, what is God's Word and His creation communicating to you . . . are you listening?

Signs We Should Discount

Signs such as bad weather, earthquakes, hurricanes, and other cataclysmic events are used today as warnings from God that He is about to come back and judge the world. To some extent these can serve as warnings, but events of these types have always occurred from time to time throughout the history of the earth. In our opinion, they act as very poor signs of the Second Coming. Only when they occur in greater frequency and magnitude and combine with other biblically confirmed signs can they communicate to us about God's return.

What we need to see instead would be events that usually occur infrequently but are happening concurrently with other signs, all recorded in our Bible. This would then mean more than an occasional earthquake or hurricane. As bad as those occasions can be, they don't mean much when they stand alone.

Given all that, one of the goals we will *not be pursuing* here in this conclusion is figuring out the exact date of Yeshua's Second Coming! Rather, our goal will be to study the signs of our day to see if they are lining up with — and beginning to fulfill — the signs of His return as found in His Word. We want to answer the question, "Is it reasonable to believe that God may very well come back in our lifetimes?" What we don't want is to be caught off guard, sleeping, and therefore not ready when He does come back.

The Shemitah Years

Recall that in our study of Daniel chapter 9 we learned that God had given His people information that would instruct them in the exact day of His first coming, Palm Sunday, or Lamb Selection Day. This was a few days before Passover. We also learned that this 70-week prophecy could be pointing at September 2015 as a time period that would correlate with the days just before the second coming of our Messiah.

What makes these time frames in the book of Daniel of interest is that 2015, along with 2022, are both *shemitah* years that start in September (or *Tishri* on the Hebrew calendar). Shemitah years are sabbatical years, occurring every seventh year. God instructed that at the end of the sabbatical year, all debts were to be eliminated and the land was to be allowed to rest. In other words, God would provide a large enough harvest in the sixth year so the people would have enough to eat for two years. The fruit and crops that would grow in the orchards and fields on their own would be available for all to freely come and harvest what they needed in that seventh year.

As Jonathan Cahn pointed out in *The Harbinger*[3] and *The Mystery of the Shemitah*[4], it seems that something both interesting and disturbing has been occurring during — and at the end of — these shemitah years. For example, 2001 and 2008 were shemitah years. The last day of the Hebrew civil year is Elul 29, which is also the last day of a shemitah year. The next day is Tishri 1, and that is the day on which the Feast of Trumpets always falls. On Elul 29, at the end of both of the last shemitah years the two worst stock market collapses occurred. Could those events be a harbinger of what might happen in 2015 and 2022? It gets more interesting if we take the shemitah years further back in time. 1994, 1987, 1980 and 1973 all had stock or bond market collapses. It seems God has been sending signals over at least the last 50 years to anyone who is listening.

We are now at the end of a set of seven increasingly earth-shattering sabbatical years. All of these years brought financial disruptions but certainly the ones in 2001 and 2008 were more extreme. These two shemitah years brought economic crises, stock market crashes, loss of jobs, and major recessions, which in the end brought the elimination of debt (one of the primary purposes of a shemitah year). With the shemitah years getting worse and worse, what judgments will fall on America and the world as the end of a shemitah year arrives in September 2015?

God may be giving us one last chance. We can either choose to bring order to our lives and usher in a time of rest and repentance, as God has instructed us to do, or God will do it Himself, mirroring the Babylonian exile. Recall that Judah, as a nation, was completely destroyed with its people exiled to a faraway land. Thus the land itself was finally allowed to rest and its disobedient people were finally removed. Individual and national debts were done away with by the total annihilation of the nation's economy. All of the people's wealth was also removed, and a state of destitution settled over the land for those who remained behind. Likewise over the next few years, our world and nation could also be judged via this same biblical principle, the law of the shemitah year.

What makes 2022 of interest is that Yom Kippur in that year comes at the end of another sabbatical year but also begins a jubilee year. All jubilee years start on Yom Kippur, ten days after Tishri 1, the civil new year on the Hebrew calendar. Keep in mind that there are several opinions as to which year is the jubilee year. However, we believe the evidence best supports 2022 as the next jubilee.

Passages in Ezekiel 1 and 40 suggest that 576 BC was a jubilee year. By adding 49 years, or multiples of 49 years, and adding back in one year because there is no year zero between 1 BC and AD 1, we arrive at 2022 as the beginning of the next jubilee year.

Jubilee years were established by God to occur at the end of every seventh sabbatical year. The end of the sabbatical year in 2022 happens to be the seventh sabbatical year in the cycle above. Thus the following year, according to God's calendar, may very well be a jubilee. The jubilee will occur, if the above assumptions are correct, on the end of this 49th year starting the 50th year with Yom Kippur in the fall and ending on the Feast of Trumpets in 2023.

Is God building to the ultimate crisis for some and a jubilee for others?

How Often Does a Jubilee Year Occur?

As a side note, biblical scholars disagree greatly over how frequent the jubilee year is. Some say that it occurs every 49 years; others say that it occurs every 50 years. We tend to believe that the jubilee year was the beginning of the next seven-year sabbatical cycle, thus making the jubilee year occur every 49th year. This makes sense if the 50th year is the first year of the next sabbatical cycle.

Understand that the estimation that the next jubilee will occur in 2022 is only that, an estimation. We believe that there is sound evidence for this date, but this evidence does not rise to the level of certainty. So we must consider these times as estimates only. I believe that God has partially hidden this knowledge from us purposely, to spur us on to study His Word and find new insights along the way. This shrouding of information does not mean that God never intends for us to discover it; it just means that He gives jewels away as they are needed.

> It is the glory of God to conceal a matter, but the glory of kings is to search out a matter. (Proverbs 25:2)

It makes perfect sense to assume that God will come back at the end of a sabbatical/jubilee time frame. In biblical terms, both of those years represent the termination of debt, or the end of the period in which we are expected to repay debt and a time in which we are to enter into a period of rest for ourselves as well as rest for the land of Israel.

In our personal lives God also gives us a time period in which to repay debt — the debt caused by our acts of disobedience. We can do that in only one way, and that is to repent of our sins and accept the price that was paid on the cross for those debts. These jubilee and sabbatical years suggest that there will come a day in which the time God has given us to repent and seek forgiveness and get our sins paid for, will come to an end. Is it coming to an end in the very near future? Yes, we think so.

What's All This About Blood Moons?

A lunar eclipse was known by the ancients as a blood moon. The moon appears blood red because, with the earth between the sun and the moon, the light coming from the sun passes through the atmosphere of the earth. Only the red light (or the red frequencies from the sun), passes through the atmosphere of the earth and is bent and hits the moon in the earth's shadow. The red rays reflect off the moon and back to the earth, during the eclipse, which makes the moon appear blood red.

What makes the year 2015 even more intriguing is that the last of four blood moons, or lunar eclipses, occur on Sukkot in 2015, fifteen days after the end of the shemitah year. And this particular blood moon isn't just any ol' blood moon – it's a super blood moon. A super blood moon occurs on September 27, 2015, meaning that the moon is at perigee, closer to the earth than at any other time of the year. It will appear 14% larger than a regular full moon. There has never been a super blood moon at the end of a shemitah year at any other time in history. This super blood moon is centered over Israel; its size and visibility make it an exclamation point as the concluding blood moon of the 2014-2015 tetrad.

Four *total* lunar eclipses occurring in a short period of time without a *partial* lunar eclipse in between is called a tetrad. Granted, a few tetrads have occurred over the last 2,000 years. But there are nine that are extremely significant, especially to Israel, because these nine tetrads have occurred on festival dates – Passover and Sukkot, the first and last of God's seven festivals and the only two which occur on a full moon. For four total lunar eclipses to fall on festival dates is rare and has only occurred eight times in the last 2,000 years. The ninth tetrad occurs in 2014 and 2015. The biblical meaning of the number nine is *completion*, *bringing to an end*, and *judgment*[5]. Is God hinting at what is about to come in the days ahead?

It seems that something important has happened to the Jews, or to the state of Israel, on each of the preceding eight tetrad occurrences. In the Talmud (which is an ancient rabbinic commentary on Torah), these blood moons were considered an omen for war. And certainly the last two tetrads fulfilled that forewarning. For example, Israel was reborn in 1948, where the end of the war in 1949 supported the eclipses that fell on 1949 and 1950. And the tetrad that occurred in 1967-68 highlighted the recapture of Jerusalem by Israel during the Six-Day War in 1967.

Israel has been re-established, Jerusalem has been regained. What's needed for prophecy to continue forward? Will the next tetrad, occurring in 2014–15, highlight the recapture of the Temple Mount and the beginning of the temple's reconstruction? We know that at least the tabernacle must be re-established before the Second Coming, because end-time events are recorded in Scripture as being fulfilled there.

Piling On?

As we await Daniel's last seven years, understand that Hebraically this time period will start at the beginning of a sabbatical period and will end at the completion of a sabbatical period. In other words, the last seven years will start on the Feast of Trumpets in 2015 or 2022 or 2029, etc.

Layer upon layer, many prophetic interpretations are lining up with what Daniel said. Daniel's prophecies might be pointing directly at 2015 and 2022 if they are interpreted as we've described above. These exact dates line up with sabbatical years, and possibly overlay the jubilee year, by adding the last week, or seven years, to the 49-year period.

God has also used the moon as a harbinger of things to come. Is it just accidental that this very rare event, in which four consecutive total lunar eclipses fall on the first and last of the seven biblical festivals, occurs with the final eclipse falling on Sukkot in 2015?

Before we leave the phenomenon of the blood moons let's make one further comment about lunar eclipses. As was brought out by the documentary *The Privileged Planet* by Gonzales and Richards[6], earth's perfect eclipses are a very rare event indeed. Most of what occurs in the galaxy when a planet's moon lines up with its sun, causing an eclipse, is that one of the following occurs: (1) the moon appears to be so much bigger than its sun that it completely covers the sun by much more that its width. (2) Or, just the opposite happens in which the moon covers only a small portion of the sun's area, making it impossible to even notice that the moon is partially in the way.

Our moon and sun are entirely unique. The sun happens to be four hundred times farther away from the earth than the moon is. But the sun also happens to be four hundred times larger than our moon, allowing them to appear the same size in our sky. So when they eclipse they almost exactly cover each other from the perspective of a person on earth. What are the odds of this occurring by accident? Why do you imagine God would create our sun and moon to appear this way?

As Gonzales and Richards propose, astronomical and earthly objects and aspects of our universe appear to be made in such a manner as to make earth the perfect platform to observe and study God's creation. If our planet, with its sun and moon, were more typical, this would not be the case. It appears that God has gone out of His way so that man can learn as much as possible. God's purpose was to allow His creation to teach man about the Creator Himself. But what many have done is to pervert the study with propositions that suggest *Chance* was our creator. Is God once again using the sun, moon, and stars as harbingers of things to come?

Approaching 6,000 Years

God has given many prophecies and hints in His Word concerning the end-time period. We'll look at two key passages, starting with Matthew:

> [24] "For false Christs and false prophets will arise and will show great signs and wonders, so as to mislead, if possible, even the elect. [25] Behold, I have told you in advance. [26] So if

they say to you, 'Behold, He is in the wilderness,' do not go out, or, 'Behold, He is in the inner rooms,' do not believe them. [27] For just as the lightning comes from the east and flashes even to the west, so will the coming of the Son of Man be. [28] Wherever the corpse is, there the vultures will gather. [29] But immediately after the tribulation of those days the sun will be darkened, and the moon will not give its light, and the stars will fall from the sky, and the powers of the heavens will be shaken. [30] And then the sign of the Son of Man will appear in the sky, and then all the tribes of the earth will mourn, and they will see the Son of Man coming on the clouds of the sky with power and great glory. [31] And He will send forth His angels with a great trumpet and they will gather together His elect from the four winds, from one end of the sky to the other. [32] Now learn the parable from the fig tree: when its branch has already become tender and puts forth its leaves, you know that summer is near." (Matthew 24:24–32)

Yeshua is telling His disciples that once the nation of Israel, referred to in the passage above as an olive tree, re-establishes itself, the generation that sees this event shall not pass away. A biblical generation is considered to be 70 to 80 years, so if we add 70 or 80 years to 1948, the year Israel became a nation again, we arrive at 2018 or 2028, certainly an interesting complement to what we've said above.

> But do not let this one fact escape your notice, beloved, that with the Lord one day is like a thousand years, and a thousand years like one day. (II Peter 3:8)

This II Peter passage is believed to hint that God has given mankind 7,000 years on the earth, with 1,000 of it represented as His 1,000-year reign. This suggests that Yeshua's Second Coming will be after the 6,000 years that started with Adam and Eve.

Bible scholars believe that the historical account of the biblical record takes the beginning back four thousand years before the birth of

Yeshua. Bishop Ussher, who lived in the 17th century AD, arrived at the date of 4004 BC for the beginning of all things. The Jewish rabbis suggest that we are in the year 5,774 from the beginning of biblical history. Several hundred years were subtracted from that accounting so as to misalign their dates with Daniel's prophecy that predicted the exact day and year of the coming of the Messiah. By adding back in those stolen two hundred years or so, their number comes very close to Bishop Ussher's date. And those totals would both suggest that we are now very close to six thousand years since the beginning of the creation.

However, even with all of the biblical and astronomical evidence coming together we are not stipulating that God is going to come back on a specific date. All we want to do here is to point out that there are many arrows that all seem to be pointing to the same time period.

Blood Moons AND Solar Eclipses

Joel 2:31, Acts 2:20, and Revelation 6:12 associate blood moons with the end times. Solar eclipses ("the sun turned black like sackcloth") are also associated with end times in each of these passages. Solar eclipses occur before each of the blood moons in 2015. A total solar eclipse occurs on March 20, 2015, at the start of Nisan 1, the first day of the biblical religious new year. God prefaced His explanation to Moses and Aaron about what to do for the Passover by stating that Nisan was to be "the beginning of months for you; it is to be the first month of the year to you" (Exodus 12:2). God uses natural phenomena to cause the sun to go dark on the first day of His religious new year. It doesn't take a genius to read into this symbolism.

Americans understand the difference between our January 1 calendar new year and the U.S. Treasury's October 1 fiscal new year. The Hebrew calendar has two new years, too. God's religious new year always starts on Nisan 1, and the civil new year starts on Tishri 1 with the celebration of the Feast of Trumpets. *In 2015 both new years are ushered in with solar eclipses.*

On our calendar, the Gregorian calendar, the days change at midnight, when most of us are asleep. On the Hebrew calendar, the days change at sundown, when the husband/father of a typical household is returning home to his family and everyone is able to welcome the new "day" together. God has reckoned days this way since the beginning: "And there was evening and there was morning, one day" (Genesis 1:5).

Saturday, March 21, 2015 is labeled Nisan 1 on Hebrew calendars. However, Nisan 1 actually began at sundown on March 20, 2015 (and some Hebrew calendars will color part of March 20 as a visual representation of this). The evening of March 20 is the beginning of Nisan 1 – and that is when the total solar eclipse occurs. Two weeks later a blood moon occurs the evening of April 4, Passover.

A half year later, a partial solar eclipse occurs on Elul 29 (the night of September 12/13, 2015), the night before Feast of Trumpets begins. This solar eclipse occurs on the last day of a very significant year – the shemitah year, the seventh year in the biblical cycle of every seven years being a sabbatical year. The last solar eclipse that occurred on Elul 29 ushered in "Black Monday" in 1987, a worse stock market crash than any single day of the 1929 crash.

Two weeks after the solar eclipse, a blood moon occurs – on September 27, 2015, the beginning of Sukkot, the last of God's seven festivals. Recall that this last blood moon of the tetrad is a super blood moon, meaning that it's larger in size. Nisan and Tishri, God's months for the religious and civil new year, both are fraught with solar eclipses followed two weeks later by blood moons in 2015.

Things Happen on the Biblical Festivals!

Significant events in Yeshua's life on earth occurred on biblical festivals. These include possibly His birth, which many suggest did not occur on Christmas but on God's festival called Sukkot. His death occurred on Passover, followed by His burial on the Feast of Unleavened Bread. His resurrection occurred on the next Sunday. And please understand that this chosen day did not signal a switch of our Lord's Day from Saturday to Sunday but instead was honoring the festival of Firstfruits. He was called the firstfruits from among the dead for good reason (I Corinthians 15:20).

Also, the Holy Spirit (our promised Comforter) came on Shavuot, or Pentecost, the fourth of the Lord's festivals. Is it any wonder that the days of the last three festivals will be involved in completing God's plan, too? Feast of Trumpets, which was a call to war, may very well usher the call to the last war, Armageddon. Yom Kippur is known as the wedding day, or judgment day, depending on your acceptance or rejection of Him. The last festival, Sukkot, celebrates the dwelling of God with man forever.

Getting Ready to Ride

What kind of upheaval comes with the astronomical signs of the solar eclipses and the blood moons? What events lie immediately ahead if our estimations are correct?

Revelation 6 is a chilling chapter describing the four horsemen of the apocalypse. These horsemen ride as each seal of a scroll is opened. In brief, these first four seals with their riders cause (1) deception, followed by (2) war, (3) economic collapse and drought (4) disease and death, with the fifth seal ushering in the (5) persecution of believers.

As a boy, when I read about the first horseman I understood that this passage was referring to spiritual deception. And I still believe that to be true. But what I was missing then was that it didn't end there. In our world today, deception is not just spiritual — it's everywhere. Wherever you look — including the media, what government officials tell us, and the reports they issue — it is becoming harder and harder to separate truth from propaganda. To make things worse, sometimes there isn't any truth at all in the reports and speeches we read and hear today.

Some Christians propose that this white horse rider is to be interpreted as the rapture of the church. But this is a very poor interpretation. Yes, our King does come back on a white horse, but not with a bow and not with the "crown" that this rider has. And He does not really conquer the earth as this rider does — God Himself simply "speaks forth" and it is so.

On the contrary, we can read all about God's Second Coming in Revelation 19. But here in chapter 6 we see an imposter, masquerading as the Real McCoy. Unfortunately, this rider will fool many.

The crown the white horse rider is flashing around is an *atarah*, the collar of a *tallit*. A tallit is a rectangular-shaped robe with an opening in the middle for the head. In accordance with God's instruction, *tzit tzit* are attached to the four corners of the tallit.

These fringes were strings woven together in such a way as to spell the name of God: YHWH. The rider in Revelation 6:2 doesn't have on a tallit like our God does when He comes back in Revelation 19; he just has the collar on. It is the showiest part, which is very telling. This deceiver is all show. Granted, he will have some power, but it will be nothing like what the Creator has and will use to put this imposter in his proper place at the end — the lake of fire.

The second horse rider is mounted on a red horse and will usher in a time of war. Some propose that this "redness" is suggesting that the Chinese or the Russians will be the instigators of war. Yes, they certainly may be involved, but the catalyst will be someone else. Remember, the key to understanding the New Testament is the Torah. And when we look into the first five books of the Old Testament, what do we find about the word "red" and who it refers to? It's none other than Esau himself.

Throughout recorded history, especially the history that God recorded for us in His Word, Esau acquired a new name because he was foolish enough to trade his birthright for a bowl of red soup. Those who first saw that trade must have been so astonished that Esau would do such a thing that they labeled him "Red." And it stuck. In the biblical text, from that point on, Esau is often referred to by the name *Edom*. This name has its root in the Hebrew word for red.

Esau is the father of the Arabs today. We believe that this worldwide war will have as its catalyst a conflict between the descendants of Esau and his brother Jacob. Jacob's descendants today are the Jews, many of whom live in Israel. Today we see wars or the beginnings of wars all over the globe. Whether it is in the Ukraine, Russia, the Mideast, or between China and Japan or other far eastern nations, it seems that all it would take for the next world war to begin is a mishandling of some geopolitical event by our leaders.

The third rider sits on a black horse. He is holding a set of scales, which symbolizes famine and economic disaster. Scales are used in the Bible to metaphorically describe someone or something that is found wanting, like Belshazzar in the book of Daniel.

> [5] Suddenly the fingers of a man's hand emerged and began writing opposite the lampstand on the plaster of the wall of the king's palace, and the king saw the back of the hand that did the writing. (Daniel 5:5)

> [25] "Now this is the inscription that was written out: 'MENE, MENE, TEKEL, UPHARSIN.' [26] This is the interpretation of the message: 'MENE'—God has numbered your kingdom and put an end to it. [27] 'TEKEL'—you have been weighed on the scales and found deficient. [28] 'PERES'—your kingdom has been divided and given over to the Medes and Persians." (Daniel 5:25–28)

In these two passages God is informing the king of Babylon that he has been weighed and found wanting, that he's "too light." God has measured Belshazzar's accomplishments in life and compared them with what God had intended for him to accomplish. And it seems that he didn't measure up, for that night the king was killed and his kingdom fell to the invading forces of the Medo-Persian Empire, led by King Cyrus.

God is also telling us that not just the kings of old will be measured, but you and I will be too. How will the weight of our works measure up? The New Testament gives further detail:

[12] Now if any man builds on the foundation with gold, silver, precious stones, wood, hay, straw, [13] each man's work will become evident; for the day will show it because it is to be revealed with fire, and the fire itself will test the quality of each man's work. [14] If any man's work which he has built on it remains, he will receive a reward. [15] If any man's work is burned up, he will suffer loss; but he himself will be saved, yet so as through fire. (1 Corinthians 3:12–15)

All of our works will be tested by fire to see if any of them measure up. Measuring up means that there are works that our Father created for us to do. It is part of His purpose and plan for each of us to behave in certain ways and accomplish certain specific goals.

Amazingly, some people will have all of their works consumed by fire, but they will still be saved because we are not saved by works but by faith. Despite this, there still seems to be a godly expectation of accomplishment for each one of us. We get to choose whether we will "measure up" or not.

Because the world will be found to be too light, God will continue to pour out his promised judgments. Those can be found in Deuteronomy 27 and 28. He warned His people that if they didn't obey His principles for holy living, certain punishments would fall on them. At the same time God also included blessings for those who would obey. But here in the sixth chapter of Revelation we see only punishment befalling mankind. Famine and economic troubles begin to spread throughout the world.

It is not hard to see signs of this very thing beginning. Never before in history have we been witness to so many nations mismanaging their currencies and spending habits. Never before have we seen so much debt that will never be paid off, except through bankruptcies – not just personal or corporate bankruptcies, but national bankruptcies as well.

What our nation — and many others — is doing has been tried before. Over the last one hundred years, many countries have mismanaged their currencies in the same way. They have printed unbacked paper money and spent it into their economies, and all such actions have had one of two results. Either they destroyed the value of their national currency, which resulted in all of their citizens losing their savings, or they destroyed the country itself. And this has not happened just in third world countries. In first world and third world alike, over the last one hundred years, all who have done what we are doing today have suffered the same result.

What is different about our day is that never before in history has the entire world printed up so much paper money in such a short period of time, paving the way for a worldwide economic collapse never before seen in the history of mankind.

Droughts and Plagues

The statistics of the National Oceanic and Atmospheric Administration (NOAA) are startling: about 50% of the continental United States is currently in drought. Most forecasters are projecting this to continue. Over 80% of California is experiencing an extreme state of dryness. This may be one of the reasons why our food prices have been going up around 7% to 9% per year lately.

And no, the true rate of inflation is not the 1.5% rate the government keeps telling us about. Some statisticians, using the formula the government used back in the early 1980s, calculate that inflation has actually been running about 9% over these last few years. This is much higher than what is being reported. If it were a country, California's production of food would rank ninth out of all the nations on earth. If the current drought is the one brought on by this black horse rider, things will get worse – much worse. Expect increases in food prices and shortages, even in America.

America is not the only place where drought is occurring. South America, parts of Africa, India, and other areas are suffering from a lack of rain. Is this the beginning of some of the effects of end-time prophecies that haven't "kicked in" completely yet? We don't know. But what is interesting is that they are all occurring at the same time.

Most Bible translations interpret the color of the fourth horse as pale. However, in both Hebrew and Greek, the word for this color is far more disturbing – a yellow-greenish color, suggesting that this horse is dead, dying, or simply putrid.

As the fourth horseman rides, an unprecedented one-fourth of the world's population will die from various pestilences, including microbial plagues. We are aware of the spread of Ebola, bringing suffering and death to thousands in western Africa. Will it infect many other countries too? No one knows. But other diseases are increasing and affecting the animals and crops we depend on.

Currently, plagues are killing hundreds of thousands of pigs in America. Terrible blights are affecting the orange crops in Florida, and the type of bananas we all enjoy are being attacked by a bug that is threatening that crop as well. Will these plagues increase or will everything settle down again? We don't know, but if these kinds of plagues continue out of control and greatly expand their reach, we may be witnessing the beginning of dangerous and difficult times.

More Seals and More Persecutions

The fifth seal ushers in persecution, exactly what we've seen increase greatly in the last few years. Christians and Jews alike are being killed for their faith, and/or their heritage, in more than 130 nations. One hundred and fifty thousand Christians were killed in 2013 alone and that number is sure to rise with the slaughtering, crucifixion, and beheading techniques being employed by the terrorists in the Middle East. It is also interesting that the very ancient slaughter technique of beheading is being brought back into use by these people. Yet it should come as no surprise to those who are students of God's Word because Revelation 20:4 predicts this very thing.

Then comes the sixth seal:

> I looked when He broke the sixth seal, and there was a great earthquake; and the sun became black as sackcloth

made of hair, and the whole moon became like blood. (Revelation 6:12)

Here we read John's ancient blood moon metaphor for a lunar eclipse and his description of a solar eclipse. He is predicting that these eclipses will occur as all the other seal events also come into full force. Are the blood moons — the tetrad that we are currently in the midst of — a fulfillment of this passage?

Continuing from the passage above, Revelation clearly reveals that these events are just the beginning of sorrows. There are many more crises to come if our projections are accurate. But they will all quickly bring us to the final events, the second coming of our Lord.

Meanwhile, are the troubling events in our current day the early signs of greater catastrophic trials ahead? Only God knows for sure. But studying His Word helps understand His warnings in advance.

Daniel Clearly Warns Us!

Much of this had to have been on Daniel's mind as he fasted and tried to learn more about the portents he received. Each of the visions lent a further understanding of the events that would befall Israel and the world, especially in their final days at the end of time.

This final generation has been warned through the writings of Daniel as well as signs in the sky and other revelations exposed by God Himself. We believe that these warnings are very similar to the warnings that God gave to Israel of old. At that time, before He would judge Israel, God always warned His people about their sinful lives and their inattention to their long-established covenant between themselves and their Creator. In those times He would remind His people of impending judgment, and I think that God is copying that pattern today.

Is it time for repentance and a return to our first love? Do certain changes need to be made in your own life? Is there a Friend who needs a bit more attention?

We think that our world, our nation, and certainly His people need to turn back to God. And when we do, it includes not just feeling sorry for the things we have done, but turning around and putting serious effort into ushering in a new lifestyle, a new way of behaving, and a new pattern to live our lives by.

This is God's calling for our day, and it's also the purpose of this book. We need to turn and choose to once again uphold the standards of God in our world, nation, and communities. But it all starts with each individual and each family. As Daniel learned, too, nothing can be accomplished if we keep the status quo. That was Daniel's greatest lesson.

What is God asking you to do to prepare for the times ahead?

How It All Fits Together

Trying to make all of these biblical numerical values line up and fit together can be exhausting and confusing. So, here in this final section I would like to give a general overview, a chronology of events that might happen if our assumptions above are true. Before we start, I would again remind the reader that as soon as we try to put God in a box, He is an expert at getting out. And so also it is true with fitting together all of these very complex details concerning end-time events found in His Word. If you have kept up to date with our writings over the years, you will have noticed that we have modified our views in small ways as more insight came into view. Certainly, the following continues in that same tradition.

Realizing that there are three approximately equal periods of time totaling about 10-1/2 years will help in setting up our timeline. Each of these periods equals about 3-1/2 years. The first 3-1/2 year period is described in these texts:

> "Now at that time Michael, the great prince who stands guard over the sons of your people, will arise. And there will be a time of distress such as never occurred since there was a nation until that time; and at that time your people,

168

everyone who is found written in the book, will be rescued." (Daniel 12:1)

Then the woman fled into the wilderness where she had a place prepared by God, so that there she would be nourished for one thousand two hundred and sixty days. (Revelation 12:6)

"And he will make a firm covenant with the many for one week, but in the middle of the week he will put a stop to sacrifice and grain offering." (Daniel 9:27a)

This first period describes Satan pursuing God's people, but God provides protection. A seven-year covenant will begin this period, and its violation will bring this 3-1/2-year period to an end. It will include the first half of the last seven years of Daniel chapter nine's seventy-week prophecy. We expect these and the following events to begin or accelerate sometime in the next few years. Wars would continue to break out and increase and have worldwide impact, but especially in and around the land of Israel. Drought, plague, and economic troubles would accelerate into full-blown crises. Persecution will also increase for the Jews as well as for all of God's people.

The second time period which immediately follows is found in these passages:

". . . but in the middle of the week he will put a stop to the sacrifice and grain offering; and on the wing of abominations will come one who makes desolate, even until a complete destruction, one that is decreed, is poured out on the one who makes desolate." (Daniel 9:27b)

"And I will grant authority to my two witnesses, and they will prophesy for twelve hundred and sixty days, clothed in sackcloth." (Revelation 11:3)

"From the time that the regular sacrifice is abolished and the abomination of desolation is set up, there will be 1,290 days." (Daniel 12:11)

There was given to him a mouth speaking arrogant words and blasphemies, and authority to act for forty-two months was given to him. (Revelation 13:5)

Then the seventh angel sounded [this is the last of the seven trumpet blasts blown in Revelation]; and there were loud voices in heaven, saying, "The kingdom of the world has become the kingdom of our Lord and of His Christ; and He will reign forever and ever." (Revelation 11:15)

Then I looked, and behold, a white cloud, and sitting on the cloud was one like a son of man, having a golden crown on His head and a sharp sickle in His hand. [15] And another angel came out of the temple, crying out with a loud voice to Him who sat on the cloud, "Put in your sickle and reap, for the hour to reap has come, because the harvest of the earth is ripe." (Revelation 14:14–15)

This second period constitutes the last half of the seven years in Daniel's seventy-week prophecy (Daniel 9:20–27). The appearance of the two witnesses begins this period and their death brings it to a close. The beast's abomination of God's temple also begins this period and brings it to a close as well. So the ending of this time period coincides with the ending of the authority of the beast (the antichrist). And as Revelation 11:15 shows, the beast's authority to rule and reign the kingdoms of the earth is over. During this time of extreme persecution, the last half of the last seven years, God's bride will be reaped from the earth and taken to safety with Him. The bride is present through the seven seal and seven trumpet events of Revelation but is taken before the bowl judgments. Other events that will occur during this 3-1/2 years will include the destruction of Gog and his armies as its forces swoop down from the lands of Russia and try to conquer the land of Israel. This war will come to a close sometime very near the beginning of this second time period. Worldwide, the lives of one-third of mankind will be lost (Revelation 9:18).

The third period of about 3-1/2 years immediately follows. Cleansing and purging of the earth will be the order of the day. The third period of time is highlighted in the following passages:

> "How blessed is he who keeps waiting and attains to the 1,335 days!" (Daniel 12:12)

> Revelation 16:1–21: The seven bowls of God's wrath.

This period begins immediately following the end of the last "week" (seven years) of Daniel. An identifying marker of this last period will be the result of the first of the seven bowls of wrath being poured out on the kingdom of the beast: loathsome and malignant sores appearing on the people who have the mark of the beast. This last time period ends with the last bowl poured out on the earth and the start of Armageddon, the last of the three end-time wars. God's bride will not witness any of these events, however, because she will be with her Groom at the end of the second 3-1/2 year time period. This scenario would imply that there will be 1,335 days of the beginning of the thousand-year reign consumed with God cleansing and purging His creation from the perversions perpetrated by the beast and those who followed his ways and were recipients of his mark.

Will our destinies be swept up in this coming storm? We will know soon enough as confirming events unfold in the immediate future. Even if some of our ideas are not quite in line or a bit more time is required for all of them to manifest, prophecy has made it abundantly evident that we live in perilous days. And those days could very well be the ones that John and Daniel warned us about. What is evident is that as the times in which we live continue to increase in turbulence, our Messiah will be at the door, ready to come for His people.

Fillings his lungs with a huge breath, Daniel took in those lovely aromas that surrounded him. The garden, much like Eden of old, was his favorite place to spend time, walking and talking with his Creator. The garden floor would make squishy noises as they walked, for the weather was perfect for nurturing all the plant life found there. All of this life seemed to radiate wonderful fragrances that Daniel's nose never seemed to become numb to. It was different than on earth where a continuous smell diminished over time, eventually seeming to go away altogether. On earth the aroma was still there. You just couldn't smell it anymore.

Here, in this garden, that never happened. In addition, the garden and its life seemed to glow. Yes, a kind of faint radiating light was emitted by all of the plants, with each different type of plant revealing a unique variation of color. Some of the colors Daniel had never seen before back on earth.

Daniel loved these walks. First, because he could spend all the time he wanted with his King. But also because he could ask questions about what was happening on earth. Because time continued here just like on earth, Daniel knew that man's time before the coming of Messiah was quickly coming to an end. Yes, he had finally figured out many more of the implications and understandings of the prophecies that God had given to him. Those were included in that scroll he had written back in Babylon on earth. Plus, God had added additional explanations during their walks together in the garden.

God told Daniel that it was all happening exactly as Daniel's scroll had foretold. These last-days' people would draw away from their Creator, being deceived by the slightest bit of subterfuge. They were not found to be good stewards of His words, and certainly not good at applying them. Many believed that most of His words had been abolished, starting some two thousand years ago.

God told him that there was a great falling away from truth. People were being deceived everywhere. But in the midst of this deception there were a few holdouts, people who still believed in the Creator as God had defined Himself. And to their credit, they also held fast to His work on the cross and the prophecies about His impending return to earth. Tears would come into his Friend's eyes and roll down His face as He revealed the final events His people would suffer. Daniel also knew a bit about the final events that these believers would endure as well.

The deception of the last days included a new idea that had arisen over the last few hundred years: believers would be taken to be with their God and Protector just before all hell would break loose. Daniel knew how harmful this belief could be, building a false hope and a false sense of security. Believers would be blinded to the need to responsibly prepare for these end-time disasters, thinking instead that they wouldn't need to do anything because they would all be gone.

Even in this lush, Eden-like paradise, sadness could be felt as they both realized the fate of those who would not be able to tell the difference between the true God and the one who was about to come, claiming the same identity. The key to identifying the real One was to know Him and His truth. The truth that doesn't change per the whims of man, and that truth's foundation was Torah.

The blood moons resonating with the portents revealed in Daniel's scroll should have alerted those still dwelling on earth to the truth. But no, many believers would fall. They would be led astray by enticing words. Words that seemed to be true, but were not, would lead them to obey and honor one who had stolen the identity and authority our enemy would soon be claiming was his.

Daniel found himself praying, once again, for these end-time believers, but this time speaking face to face with the only One who could save.

Endnotes

Chapter 1: An Overview

[1] The Old Testament refers to Asherah poles 39 times. For example: Exodus 24:13, Deuteronomy 7:5, Deuteronomy 12:3, Deuteronomy 16:21, Judges 6:25, I Kings 14:23, II Kings 23:6, Isaiah 27:9, Jeremiah 17:2, Micah 5:14.

Chapter 2: The Statue

[1] John Klein and Adam Spears, with Michael Christopher, Volume 1, Lost in Translation, Rediscovering the Roots of Our Faith (Bristol, TN: Selah Publishing Group, 2007), pp. 99–117.

[2] http://jewishencyclopedia.com/articles/1440-amraphel.

[3] John Klein and Adam Spears, with Michael Christopher, Volume 3, Lost in Translation, Two Brides, Two Destinies (Bristol, TN: Selah Publishing Group, 2012), p. 162–165.

Chapter 3: The Tree

[1] http://jewishencyclopedia.com/articles/4871-daniel.

[2] H. W. F. Gesenius, Gesenius' Hebrew-Chaldee Lexicon to the Old Testament (Grand Rapids, MI: Baker Book House, 1979), ref. no. 5019.

[3] http://www.20000-names.com/origin_of_baby_names/etymology_B_male/meaning_of_the_name_belteshazzar.htm.

[4] Gesenius, Gesenius' Hebrew-Chaldee Lexicon to the Old Testament, ref. no. 1078.

[5] Ibid., ref. no. 1095.

[6] Ibid., ref. no. 5894.

[7] James Strong, Strong's Exhaustive Concordance of the Bible: Updated Edition (Peabody, MA: Hendirckson Publishers, Inc., 2009), ref. no. 3825.

Chapter 4: The Handwriting on the Wall

[1] http://jewishencyclopedia.com/articles/2846-belshazzar.

[2] H. W. F. Gesenius, Gesenius' Hebrew-Chaldee Lexicon to the Old Testament (Grand Rapids, MI: Baker Book House, 1979), ref. no 1.

[3] https://www.youtube.com/watch?v=7gZYB1m3-T0.

[4] Ibid.

Chapter 5: The Four Beasts

[1] H. W. F. Gesenius, *Gesenius' Hebrew-Chaldee Lexicon to the Old Testament* (Grand Rapids, MI: Baker Book House, 1979), ref. no. 704.

² Ibid., ref. no. 2166.
³ James Strong, *Strong's Exhaustive Concordance of the Bible: Updated Edition* (Peabody, MA: Hendirckson Publishers, Inc., 2009), ref. no. 2165.
⁴ Gesenius, *Gesenius' Hebrew-Chaldee Lexicon to the Old Testament*, ref. no. 1882.

Chapter 7: The Seventy-Week Prophecy

1 http://www.gracecentered.com/christian_forums/theology/*1*2*3*does-god-have-a-redemptive-clock*4*5*6*/5/?wap2 .
² James Strong, Strong's Exhaustive Concordance of the Bible: Updated Edition (Peabody, MA: Hendirckson Publishers, Inc., 2009), ref. no. 7620.
³ H. W. F. Gesenius, Gesenius' Hebrew-Chaldee Lexicon to the Old Testament (Grand Rapids, MI: Baker Book House, 1979), ref. no. 226.
⁴ Ibid., ref. no. 4150.
⁵ Strong, Strong's Exhaustive Concordance of the Bible: Updated Edition, ref. no. 3467.
⁶ John Klein and Adam Spears, with Michael Christopher, Volume 1, Lost in Translation, Rediscovering the Roots of Our Faith (Bristol, TN: Selah Publishing Group, 2007), p. 30–31.

Chapter 8: Angelic Warfare

¹ H. W. F. Gesenius, *Gesenius' Hebrew-Chaldee Lexicon to the Old Testament* (Grand Rapids, MI: Baker Book House, 1979), ref. no. 8269.
² Ibid., ref. no. 1966.
³ James Strong, *Strong's Exhaustive Concordance of the Bible: Updated Edition* (Peabody, MA: Hendirckson Publishers, Inc., 2009), ref. no. 2398.

Chapter 9: The Antichrist and His Archetype, Antiochus

¹ http://en.wikipedia.org/wiki/Antiochus_IV_Epiphanes.

Chapter 10: The Final Beast

¹ H. W. F. Gesenius, *Gesenius' Hebrew-Chaldee Lexicon to the Old Testament* (Grand Rapids, MI: Baker Book House, 1979), ref. no. 1860.
² Ibid., ref. no. 7919.
³ Ibid., ref. no. 1847.

Chapter 11: Prophetic Signs in Our Times

¹ H. W. F. Gesenius, *Gesenius' Hebrew-Chaldee Lexicon to the Old Testament* (Grand Rapids, MI: Baker Book House, 1979), ref. no. 226.
² John Klein with Michael Christopher, *Anatomy of the Heavens: God's Message in the Stars* (Bristol, TN: Selah Publishing Group, 2013).
³ Jonathan Cahn, *The Harbinger* (Lake Mary, FL: Charisma House, 2012).

Endnotes

[4]Jonathan Cahn, *The Mystery of the Semitah* (Lake Mary, FL: Frontline Charisma Media/Charisma House Book Group, 2014).

[5] E. W. Bullinger, *Number in Scripture* (Grand Rapids, MI: Kregel Publications, 1967), p. 235.

[6] Guillermo Gonzales and Jay Richards, *The Privileged Planet: How Our Place in the Cosmos is Designed for Discovery* (Washington DC: Regnary Publishers, 2004). This is also the name of a video put together by the same authors and available at privilegedplanet.com.

Bibliography

Aharoni, Yohanan. (1962). *The Land of the Bible.* Philadelphia, PA: Westminster Press.

Aharoni, Yohanan & Avi-Yonah, Michael. (1968). *The MacMillan Bible Atlas.* New York, NY: MacMillan Publishing.

Biltz, Mark. (2014). *Blood Moons: Decoding the Imminent Heavenly Signs* New York, NY: Midpoint Trade Books.

Biven, David & Blizzard, Roy, Jr. (2001). *Understanding the Difficult Words of Jesus.* Shippensburg, PA: Destiny Image.

Black, Naomi (Ed.). (1989). *Celebration: The Book of Jewish Festivals.* Middle Village, NY: Jonathan David Publications, Inc.

Bullinger, E. W. (1967). *Number in Scripture.* Grand Rapids, MI: Kregel Publications.

Cahn, Jonathan. (2011). *The Harbinger.* Lake Mary, FL: FrontLine Charisma Media/Charisma Book Group.

Cahn, Jonathan. (2014). *The Mystery of the Shemtah.* Lake Mary, FL: Frontline Charisma Media/Charisma House Book Group.

Church, J. R. & Stearman, Gary. (1993). *The Mystery of the Menorah* Oklahoma City, OK: Prophecy Publications.

Cohen, Abraham A. (1995). *Everyman's Talmud: The Major Teachings of the Rabbinic Sages.* New York, NY: Schocken Books.

Cohen, Shaye J. D. (1987). *From the Maccabees to the Mishnah.* Philadelphia, PA: The Westminster Press.

Edersheim, Alfred. (2000). *The Life and Times of Jesus the Messiah.* Peabody, MA: Hendrickson Publishers, Inc.

Edersheim, Alfred. (1994). *Sketches of Jewish Social Life*. Peabody, MA: Hendrickson Publishers, Inc.

Edersheim, Alfred. (1994). *The Temple: Its Ministry and Services*. Peabody, MA: Hendrickson Publishers, Inc.

Friedman, David. (2001). *They Loved the Torah*. Baltimore, MD: Lederer Books.

Frydland, Rachmiel. (1991). *What Rabbis Know About the Messiah*. Columbus, OH: Messianic Literature Outreach.

Gesenius, H. W. F. (1979). *Gesenius' Hebrew-Chaldee Lexicon to the Old Testament*. Grand Rapids, MI: Baker Book House.

Goodwin, Mark. (2013, 2014). *America's Exit Strategy*. Fort Lauderdale, FL: Goodwin America Corp.

Howard, Kevin, and Rosenthal, Marvin. (1997). *The Feasts of the Lord*. Orlando, FL: Zion's Hope, Inc., Thomas Nelson.

Kasdan, Barney. (1993). *God's Appointed Times: A Practical Guide for Understanding and Celebrating the Biblical Holidays*. Baltimore, MD: Messianic Jewish Publishers.

Kohlenberger, John R, III. (1979). *The Interlinear NIV Hebrew English Old Testament*. Grand Rapids, MI: Zondervan Publishing.

McKee, J.R. (2012). *One Law for All*. Kissimmee, FL: TNN Press.

Middelkoop, Willem. (2014). *The Big Reset*. Chicago, IL: Amsterdam University Press.

Mortimer, Susan. (2007). *A Complete Guide to Celebrating Our Messiah in the Festivals*. Duncan, OK: Eagle's Wings Educational Materials.

Lash, Jamie. (1997). *The Ancient Jewish Wedding . . . and the Return of Messiah for His Bride*. Ft. Lauderdale, FL: Jewish Jewels.

Schiff, Peter. (2012). *The Real Crash: America's Coming Bankruptcy*. New York, NY: St. Martin's Press.

Scott, Bruce. (1997). *The Feasts of Israel*. Bellmawr, NJ: Friends of Israel Gospel Ministry.

Seekins, Frank T. (1994). *Hebrew Word Pictures*. Phoenix, AZ: Living-Word Pictures, Inc.

Shanks, Hershel. (1992). *Understanding the Dead Sea Scrolls*. New York, NY: Random House.

Stern, David H. (1990). *Restoring the Jewishness of the Gospel*. Clarksville, MD: Jewish New Testament Publications, Inc.

Strassfield, Michael. (1985). *The Jewish Holidays: A Guide and Commentary*. New York, NY: Harper Row Publishers, Inc.

Strong, James. (2009). *Strong's Exhaustive Concordance of the Bible: Updated Edition*. Peabody, MA: Hendirckson Publishers, Inc.

Ussher, James. (2003). *The Annals of the World*. Green Forest, AR: Master Books, Inc.

Wilkerson, David. (1998). *America's Last Call: On the Brink of Financial Holocaust*. Lindale, TX: Wilkerson Trust Publications.

Wilkerson, David. (1976). *Racing Toward Judgment*. Old Tappan, NJ: Fleming H. Revell Co.

Wilkerson, David (1974). *The Vision*. Old Tappan, NJ: Fleming H. Revell Co.

Wilson, Marvin R. (1989). *Our Father Abraham*. Grand Rapids, MI: Wm. B. Eerdmans Publishing Co.

Zimmerman, Martha. (1981). *Celebrate the Feasts*. Minneapolis, MN: Bethany Fellowship, Inc.

Other Books

Lost in Translation: Rediscovering the Hebrew Roots of our Faith (*Volume 1*)

John Klein and Adam Spears

Despite the sensational nature of its subject, *Lost in Translation: Rediscovering the Hebrew Roots of our Faith* is written in simple, clear, rational language that relies 100 percent on the Bible as the ultimate authority. The authors shed light on centuries of confusion surrounding subjects that are seldom addressed in modern sermons and Bible studies.

Using ancient Hebrew language and culture, the authors clarify many of the Bible's so-called "mysteries" and help the reader uncover the treasure of foundational truths that have been "lost in translation." Topics include:

- Who is the Bride of Messiah?
- Is there a difference between covenant and testament?
- How does the rainbow reflect God's plan for mankind?
- What is the difference between devils, demons, and Nephilim?

Join us on an exciting adventure to rediscover the treasures still buried within the pages of The Book that reveal the pathway to the heart of God.

Lost in Translation: The Book of Revelation through Hebrew Eyes (*Volume 2*)

John Klein and Adam Spears

The Book of Revelation through Hebrew Eyes is the second in the Lost in Translation three-volume series. The title says it all! This book takes a look at the first half of the book of Revelation from its Hebraic cultural and linguistic perspective. The truth of many misunderstood

183

verses will be revealed when the light of ancient Hebrew interpretation is shone on the Bible's premiere book of end-time prophecy.

Many intriguing questions will be answered, such as:

- Who are the 144,000?
- Are all believers the Bride of Messiah?
- What are the locusts that come from the abyss?

If you're interested in end-time prophecy, we highly recommend reading the first volume of this series, because it lays the foundation for understanding the book of Revelation.

Lost in Translation: The Book of Revelation: Two Brides — Two Destinies (Volume 3)

John Klein and Adam Spears

In the final volume of this series the authors explore the second half of Revelation from the perspective of a Hebrew God speaking through a Hebrew believer to an audience that was intimately familiar with the Hebrew language, culture, customs, and concepts that form both the literal and metaphorical foundation for vast portions of Revelation. In the process they answer a multitude of important questions, including:

- Whose bride are you? Can you change sides or are you stuck forever in a relationship you really don't want?
- Who or what is the False Messiah? The False Prophet?
- What is the Second Death?

Could these catastrophes happen in my lifetime?
It is especially important for the current generation to understand the Bible's premiere book on end-time prophecy because deception will be rampant.

Anatomy of the Heavens, God's Message in the Stars

John Klein

The constellations in our night sky have captivated almost everyone throughout history and have a remarkable story to tell. It's God's most dramatic message, and it's literally written in the stars. Each of the 12 constellations plays its part in telling the overarching plan God has had since the beginning of creation.

Although Satan has used astrology to pervert God's purpose for the stars, God has provided the starry hosts to fulfill the reason for their creation. The stars were originally created for signs (Genesis 1:14) — signs which link to biblical prophecy. Each of the 12 tribes is represented and embellished by one of the constellations. Amazingly, the position of the stars during the biblical festivals also gives insight into God's grand plan.

Family Sabbath Seder

Jodi Klein

The *Family Sabbath Seder* makes it easy for your family to join together in marking the beginning and closing of Sabbath, setting it off as the best day of the week. The Seder contains well-thought-out gems that have been developed by people over the centuries to aid in keeping the fourth commandment. Candle lighting, wine, bread, and havdalah blessings are in easy-to-read Hebrew transliterations so your family can correctly pronounce the Hebrew if you decide to use the Hebrew blessings. Our tried-and-true favorite hallah bread recipes are included (with one for bread machines!) along with a question and answer page, geared to pointing out that everything you do in welcoming the Sabbath is imbued with meaning.

The Family Sabbath Seder makes it easy to establish rich traditions that will continue for generations.

Couple's Sabbath Seder

Jodi Klein

This Seder is a tool for couples to use in welcoming the Sabbath. Included are candle lighting, wine, bread, and havdalah blessings in easy-to-read Hebrew transliterations and our favorite hallah bread recipes. The Seder will fulfill any couple's desire to please God by marking the opening and closing of the Sabbath in this special way.

Single's Sabbath Seder

Jodi Klein

Begin your Sabbath by reflecting on God with these time-honored traditions adapted specifically for the single person. You're invited to meet with Him as His special day arrives, and a tradition of using the *Sabbath Seder* can enrich that intimate weekly appointment.

Hanukkah Covenant Seder

Jodi Klein

This family-friendly Seder takes you through the eight nights of Hanukkah by beginning with a Hebrew blessing centering on Yeshua and transliterated phonetically so that even those unfamiliar with Hebrew can read it accurately. This Seder is unique in that it uses color to teach about covenant and to answer the question, "How do I draw near to God?" Each night includes sections on covenant, relevant scriptures, enrichment, and the history of Hanukkah, enabling kids and adults to understand covenant and what it means to have a relationship with the Light of the World. This 60-page booklet is chock full of suggestions to make your Hanukkah more meaningful than ever.

S'firat HaOmer: Counting the Omer

Jodi Klein

Leviticus 23:15–16 instructs us to count the omer. How do we do that? This book makes it simple, with one page for each day of the count. The short blessing and the count are in Hebrew and English, with easy to pronounce phonetic Hebrew. Counting the Omer is 100% user-friendly: if you can read English, you can correctly pronounce the Hebrew transliteration! We have not seen another book that makes it so easy for you to fulfill the Leviticus 23:15–16 command, and you'll end up learning some Hebrew while you're at it.

Why did God instruct us to count up seven weeks to Shavuot beginning on the festival of Firstfruits? Because the wheat harvest, Shavuot, is the best harvest and represents the Groom's harvest of the Bride. There's going to be a wedding! Shavuot (Pentecost in Greek) represents the Hebrew custom of the snatching of the Bride prior to the wedding. Counting the Omer is the intense anticipation God built into this particular holiday by requiring us to count the days leading up to it.

The Key to Your Weather Forecast

John Klein

Talk of the current weather forecast is one of the most common but least understood topics. This book will cut through all the confusion and allow anyone to make an accurate weather forecast. Used in a remote outdoor location or just around town, this field guide will enable you to quickly acquire an understanding of what causes the dramatic weather changes, which we all talk about, and make your own exciting predictions.

This key has been designed to make weather forecasting fun and easy and distinguishes this book from every other on the subject. Without the need for prior instruction or aid, you can determine the weather by answering the simple questions in the key. The promise: this book will enable you to accurately forecast the weather for the next few days in about five minutes.